Legal and Disclaimer Notice
Liability: Although every effort has been made to present the experience, expertise, and information shared in this book with accuracy of the content within, the authors and publisher assume no responsibility for any errors, omissions, or damage caused or alleged to be caused, directly or indirectly, by this content.

The advice and information provided are general, and cannot apply to every individual situation. Consequently, your goals and the details of your business should be reviewed with professionals you authorize to provide guidance in your specific case and particular circumstance.

Your use of the content herein, intended for informational purposes only, means you will not hold the authors, their organizations, or any entities with which they are affiliated responsible or legally liable for any errors, omissions, or inaccuracies. With seeking the advice of qualified professionals for your specific circumstance, when you deem it necessary, you must ensure you comply and adhere to the laws that govern your business, industry, local area, region, and country. These include the set of privacy-relative ones such as General Data Privacy Regulations (GDPR).

Library of Congress Control Number: 2020936506

ISBN 978-0-9990823-7-9
Published 2020 | First printing
Published simultaneously in electronic format
REBRAND Publishing™
24 Corliss Street No. 6791
Providence, RI 02940 USA

Connect with REBRAND™ at REBRAND.com | linkedin.com/company/REBRAND

REBRAND

Transform to Thrive™
Where the world goes for winning brands.
We publish, showcase, and advise C-suite experts and global leaders driving brand change.

DATA POINTS GOLD

Create, Curate, and Monetize Your Information Assets

STRATEGIES FOR A BRANDED BENCHMARK BREAKTHROUGH

ANAEZI MODU | ANZIYA BUNDU

ACKNOWLEDGEMENTS

For our loving family, from the youngest to the oldest, and those that left us much earlier than we had hoped. Thank you for your continued support, advice, and much more. We wouldn't have taken on this particular challenge without your encouragement every step of the way.

For our friends and colleagues, thank you for the many ways you have contributed to our finally starting and finishing this essential guide.

Most importantly, we thank God for his past, present, and continued blessings in all the challenges and initiatives we embrace.

CONTENTS

PART 1:
A BRANDED BENCHMARK SUCCESS STORY 2

What Does It Cost to Rebrand? 2

What Might Compete with Brand for Top Position? 5

What is a Benchmark? 7
A Super Simple Benchmark:
The Barbara Corcoran Story 8

Why are Benchmarks Important? 9

Who Uses Branded Benchmarks? 9

How to Benefit from Your Own Branded Benchmark 10
The New Marketing Landscape 11
Branding, Naming, Positioning, Media 12
Cutting Through the Content Clutter 13
Customers and Clients Are in Charge 15
Information with Actionable Insights
is the New Currency 16

Types of Branded Benchmarks 18

PART 2:
GETTING STARTED WITH BENCHMARKING 22

Internally Focused Data Collection 23
Externally Focused Methods 24

How to Choose a Benchmark Focus 24
Explore Popular Topic Areas 25
Review the Preferences of Your Ideal Client 25
Harvest Information Gaps 26
Ask Clients or Your Community
What They Want to Know 26

Keep Benchmarking Affordable 27
Start Small 27
Stay Focused 28
Cut Costs or Piggyback Information 29

Roadmap to a Successful Benchmark 30
1. Define Your Why 31
2. Establish a Compelling Topic 31
3. Design a Methodology 32
4. Compile the Data 32
5. Summarize Your Results 33
6. Partner, Promote and Market 33
7. Follow Up, Evolve, and Extend 34

PART 3:
MARKET YOUR BRANDED BENCHMARK 36

Naming and Positioning 37

Create a Microsite for the Branded Benchmark 37
Special Note: Importance of Privacy 38

Package the Benchmark 38

The Importance of Design......40

Promote on Social Media......40

Harness the Power of Public Relations......41
Media kit......42
Events......43
Networking......46

Printed Pieces......47

Market Through Amazon......48

PART 4: POSITION YOUR BENCHMARK AS A BRAND......50

Brand Consistency vs. Coherence......52

Mobile Matters......52

Naming......53

Onlyness......56
Onlyness Exercise and Examples......57

Visual Identity......59

PART 5: CASE EXAMPLES OF BRANDED BENCHMARKS......64

Architecture Billings Index......65
Big Mac Index......67
BUILDPLAY Digital Index™......68
Edelman Trust Barometer......71
Fast Company Innovation by Design Awards......73
Interbrand Best Global Brands......75

Landor M&A Brand Study 77
Mijks Digital Airport Index 79
Prophet Brand Relevance Index® 82
REBRAND 100® Global Awards 84
Simplicity Index 86
T+L Top 500 89
TeenBusiness® Top 20 92
The State of Fashion 93
Twiplomacy 95
VIM Group ImpactValuator™ 97
World Architecture 100 99
World Value Index 101

NEXT STEPS TO GET STARTED 106

BONUS RESOURCES 109

GLOSSARY 112

REFERENCES 120

ABOUT THE AUTHORS 122

ABOUT REBRAND 124

YOUR NOTES 125

PART 1

"Benchmarking can help any business, big or small, boost visibility, build credibility, find innovative ways to serve clients, and, eventually, break the revenue glass ceiling."

A BRANDED BENCHMARK SUCCESS STORY

What Does it Cost to Rebrand?

In considering this question, the investment to hire brand consultants usually comes to mind. But what's required to implement the rebrand is overlooked or underestimated.

As a result, companies do not factor the true costs of rebranding. They often find themselves forced to cut corners and make compromises during implementation. This can result in weakening the effectiveness of the rebrand.

This was a problem that VIM Group observed after working on 1,200+ projects over 27 years. The company is the global leader in managing the change of all brand touchpoints of their clients around the world, found at vim-group.com.

To enable their clients to accurately budget and scope their rebranding, they reviewed the implementation data they compiled over the years. They then assessed the financial, organizational, visual, and digital consequences of implementation. These assessments pertained to project types that included M&A (mergers and acquisitions) or change in business model.

> The result was ImpactValuator™ with its key finding that can be summed up in a simple ratio: 1:20

That is, the ratio between the fees for brand and design consultants compared to the cost for implementation is 1 to 20.

If an organization spends $1 million to restructure their brand, it will cost $20 million to implement the change in spaces, on documents, uniforms, and all physical and digital touchpoints.

> Note: A touchpoint is wherever clients, customers, employees, investors, the community, and the general public come in contact or interact with a brand. These touchpoints can be online or offline, and can pertain to the five senses of sight, sound, taste, smell, touch.

With the aptly named and trademarked ImpactValuator™ VIM Group's clients can accurately estimate the potential cost of brand implementation and identify areas for cost savings. They can also consider different rollout scenarios and choose the one that best aligns with their goals and resources.

The tool and corresponding services of ImpactValuator have been smartly positioned as an important sub-brand of VIM Group. Clients and others access the information and insights it provides directly or as part of VIM Group's consulting services.

ImpactValuator is an example of a branded benchmark that establishes expertise, attracts clients, and helps boost profits.

> "ImpactValuator is an example of a branded benchmark that establishes expertise, attracts clients, and helps boost profits."

Aside from its practical usefulness, ImpactValuator has also helped solidify VIM Group's position as the founder of the brand implementation category. The result has been that VIM Group plays a much higher, strategic, and consultative role with global brands like Siemens, Deutsche Telekom, DHL, SkyTeam, and IKEA.

But the power of branded benchmarks doesn't belong only to large corporations and organizations.

Thanks to the long arm of social media and the ease of data analysis today, big corporations no longer have a lock on data generation. Small businesses, startups and non-profits also have access to some of the same secret weapons that big companies leverage: branded benchmarks developed from data and information assets.

Benchmarking can help any business, big or small, to boost their visibility, build credibility, find innovative ways to serve clients, and eventually, break the revenue glass ceiling.
No doubt about it. Developing your valuable branded benchmark can affect your company's bottom line.

"The portion of corporate market value attributable to intangibles grew from 17% in 1975 to a whopping 81% in 2010," as Doug Laney, author of the ground-breaking book, *Infonomics*, cited based on research by Ocean Tomo in his article titled *Tobin's Q+A: Evidence of Information's Real Market Value*[1]. Although more recent information is not currently available, there's a likelihood the percentage is higher today.

And what are these intangibles? Brand consultants would put *brand* at the top of that list of valuable assets.

What Might Compete with Brand for Top Position?

Information. Data. Insights.

"Info savvy organizations enjoy a market to book value that's nearly two times higher than the market average," Laney says.

Indeed, information accumulation has not only dramatically increased in businesses, it will continue to accelerate in our everyday lives, thanks to technological developments. One such development is the internet of things or IoT, in which many devices will be connected to the internet to receive and send information. Imagine your refrigerator, once it realizes that you're low on eggs, communicating with the inventory database of your favorite grocery store to order your brand of free-range, omega 3-enriched eggs—and letting you know when it's available.

> "Info savvy organizations enjoy a market to book value that's nearly two times higher than the market average."

5G internet promises to be up to 50% faster than 4G, which can only mean even faster access to information. Machine Learning and Artificial Intelligence (AI), which we're already experiencing first-hand in the form of Amazon's recommendation engine, for example, generate enormous volumes of information used by businesses and buyers alike.

The point is, data is being generated through various sources, and it's perceived as an asset, not just in business, but in daily living. Learning and leveraging the opportunities revealed from that data is important, while respecting growing concerns and policies about personal privacy.

> "Data is being generated through various sources, and it's perceived as an asset, not just in business, but in daily living."

Those who harness and organize the data to extract insights and make them actionable add even more value. In fact, the importance of information itself has supplanted traditional assets in generating revenue, thereby contributing to market value as well.

Every business has the means to generate original data and insights of interest to others. You don't have to consult or outsource to develop valuable, branded information assets yourself. Developing your own distinct benchmark is within your reach, even if you're a small or one-person firm.

Identifying and initiating a proprietary, unique, data-rich benchmark can cost as little as company time and attention. Research you conduct on your own initiative counts. So does a survey you design and implement to learn something new and specific. Competitions or awards programs you run internally or externally can also generate information and rankings that are types of benchmarks.

If you don't want to or can't generate your own data, you can build on already existing information, such as what you can find in the public domain and through free government sources. You can also enhance information or data others generate, in partnership or in alliance with them.

If you are a solopreneur with a significant social media following, you likely have free, valuable data at your fingertips that the platforms provide. With some focus and guidance, there are valuable insights you can leverage to increase revenue for your brand, share to boost your authority, or market to others.

What Is a Benchmark?

Benchmarking refers to tracking quantitative or qualitative data process measurements or information that can help gauge actionable insights, offer guidance, or inspire improvement. A benchmark can reveal best in class examples for internal or external change.

With that definition, an index, periodic survey, ranking, or industry recognitions and competitions can be considered benchmarks. Simply put, a benchmark is any type of qualitative or quantitative set of information that provides actionable insights and drives decisions. It tracks performance metrics and best practices tied to business achievement.

"Benchmarking refers to tracking quantitative or qualitative data process measurements or information that can help gauge actionable insights, offer guidance, or inspire improvement."

A benchmark is reached by measuring an aspect of a company product, service, or procedure, often comparing it with those of entities considered to be best in class. The gap between the two can reveal the areas and possible processes to improve within the company as well as outside in the marketplace.

For instance, one study could compare how the largest or smallest companies in your city, state or industry engage on social media in general or LinkedIn specifically. We, in fact, conducted this study for the A/E/C (architecture, engineering and construction) industry for BUILDPLAY, a member of the REBRAND Alliance. You'll read more about that later.

Another example is running a one-off comparison within your industry to provide value, garner attention, or create a starting point for an ongoing effort. Many will learn from that.

A Super Simple Benchmark:
The Barbara Corcoran Story

Barbara Corcoran, the former New York City real estate entrepreneur (now part of Shark Tank as of this writing), tells a story about a simple, bold PR move she made using the simplest data. We paraphrase here:

She once had 11 condos for sale. She averaged the cost of those listings and sent a note to publications stating that the average cost for condos in New York City was that number.

Journalists ran with the information, sparking interest about the industry and generating welcome media coverage for her growing firm.

This is an example of how an important, unique or fascinating bit of information for the right audience can drive attention and credibility. As you can imagine, that exposure and becoming perceived as a source of helpful information and insights garnered Corcoran even more attention and more customers.

She certainly didn't make any misleading claims about how she arrived at her conclusion. It was probably done in fun, and worth the effort for the much-needed attention boost to her business at that time.

Why Are Benchmarks Important?

Tracking actionable information can help your business grow by offering a gauge for future goals and the means to achieve them. Used internally, benchmarks can reveal ways to increase efficiency, cut costs, improve customer experiences and more.

When you track data and glean insights about your company's performance, you might find other ways to use benchmarks to a market advantage. You can also build a new revenue stream by marketing the information assets to those who need and value them.

Both internal or external applications for benchmarks can be built upon to create a body of benchmarking information whose value will increase over time. If you are tracking information that compares companies in your city, once you have gathered the information, you could do it again after 12 or 24 months.

You will then be able to share differences between the two collection periods. If you continue in subsequent years, this will make the benchmark more valuable as the years accumulate. You can now note the direction of trends and possibly generate predictive analytics—your projected assumptions on future dates, based on the data and information gathered, over time.

Who Uses Branded Benchmarks?

Reliable data with value-added insights from a respected company is of great benefit for many organizations. Want to know how your virtual file storage company can gain ground in the cloud industry? Access answers in various IBM benchmark reports by searching on Google or at ibm.com.

Want to learn about women-owned businesses? There is data on that from searching on Google, or researching through the Small Business Administration (SBA) in the US, or its counterparts in many countries around the world.

Ask yourself who might want and need your valuable information. If your company sells outdoor clothing and you regularly survey your customers, who could benefit from that information? Organizations that serve hikers, bikers, or climbers, for example, could be a start.

Suppose you further survey those organizations for correlations with your original data. You might reveal the health impact of various outdoor activities and draw demographic connections. Major health care and drug research-and-development entities may then gain from your studies.

As you might imagine, anyone from customers, vendors, industry players (including competitors), and complementary industries may find a benchmark useful. If you position it with some elements used to position a brand, you'll be remembered, respected, and attract prospects that could convert to paying clients or customers.

In **Part 5**, we review a list of various types of benchmarks. The descriptions of their methodologies and other information might inspire you to create your own.

How to Benefit from Your Own Branded Benchmark

You can imagine why reports on topics mentioned above would be of interest to various companies. They can apply to those in adjacent sectors seeking new marketplace opportunities.

We've already established that your business can generate useful, actionable information, either internally, in contrast to competitors, or on behalf of a targeted customer/client industry, from which you would like to receive attention.

You can also take research compiled by others, such as a study of top 100 US employers, and enhance it with new analysis and conclusions. Doing so could turn it into proprietary information under your brand.

> "Your business can generate useful, actionable information, either internally, in contrast to competitors, or on behalf of a targeted customer/ client industry"

Either way, this information benefits your business. You can use it internally to make your business more effective, efficient, and profitable. Externally, your branded benchmark brings you attention and positions you as an authority in your industry. You can also sell the full report of your study, giving you another revenue stream.

Let's look more closely at where a branded benchmark can take your business.

- **The New Marketing Landscape**
  Traditional hit-or-miss ads are out. Marketing today must share content that is helpful and relevant, addressing specific issues. In fact, the new way to "market" is to advise and to educate long before a prospect might be inspired to reach out to you. Social media continues to become ever more popular and far-reaching, providing both new opportunities and challenges as channels essential to spreading that useful information and content.

  While marketing has always been about influencing how and when people think about a product or service, today's strategies use big data and algorithms to increase the psychological impact on consumers. Think of the "if you liked x, you might like y" angle that Machine Learning tools have helped make possible. Internet pop-up ads match your recent topic searches, since the data "learns" your interests and shopping behaviors. These are more effective ways to get a prospect's attention than blanket ads that are ignored.

- **Branding, Naming, Positioning, Media**
  Branding takes you even farther than marketing campaigns can. It is the essence of your organization, within which is the core purpose and reasoning behind why you exist and whom you serve.

  That core can inform the expertise and authority you're known for, which a strategic benchmark can help you establish and strengthen.

"Branding takes you even farther than marketing campaigns can. It is the essence of your organization"

"Marketing is about getting customers. Branding is about keeping them," says Marty Neumeier, renowned author and brand strategist.

Since it's easier than ever to start a business, you're now competing with far more than industry leaders. There is an increasing number of new entrants whose novelty can be a draw for prospects.

Not so long ago, establishing an online presence and asserting your brand only meant creating a website and filling it with keyword-rich content. This was enough to get ranked on search engines so that site visitors could discover your company. It was also easier to generate leads from traffic referred from Facebook, Twitter, Instagram, LinkedIn, and other social media platforms.

Once these became established, marketers and your prospects faced another roadblock: **content overwhelm**.

- **Cutting Through the Content Clutter**
  We're drowning in an ocean of content clutter about countless topics and from as many sources: social media posts... reports... graphics... email newsletters... podcasts... videos... and much more. Even content about our areas of interest are making us numb by their sheer volume.

  Much like a string of pushy television commercials, the abundance of online pieces has diluted the effectiveness of even the most value-infused content. An article on your website must compete with similar content on countless other websites. And so, **even the most brilliant, unique ideas and messages can be lost in this space.**

  How can you rise above the noise and cut through the content clutter?

  "The answer is simple," wrote Andy Crestodina, speaker and co-founder of Orbit Media Studios, "create a survey that produces new data. The Internet wants originality. It's the original research that gets clicked, read and shared."[2] This is why Crestodina believes the 150+ hours they spend on their annual blogger survey is more than worthwhile.

  > "Benchmarking puts statistical weight behind your message—and makes your target audience more likely to listen."

  When content has a reduced impact, unique and original information with actionable insights speak more loudly. Benchmarking puts statistical weight behind your message—and makes your target audience more likely to listen. Valuable and compelling insights from data you either create or curate still cuts through that content clutter. The information you have or continually generate is a valuable asset, no matter your company size or industry. This recognition has deepened interest in ways to market and monetize this information.

Small businesses don't have to miss out on opportunities that information assets can provide to the bottom line. In fact, there are exciting ways for small to mid-sized businesses to benefit.

> "The information you have or continually generate is a valuable asset, no matter your company size or industry."

This holds true even if you don't generate the data yourself. Hundreds, if not thousands of information assets exist publicly through taxpayer-supported research. At least an equal number of companies make their data available to build trust, credibility, and authority in their areas of focus.

If you don't have the resources to conduct your own original research, you can access publicly-available information to enhance or incorporate in some meaningful way. With a little creativity and ingenuity, however you gather or access data, the results can lead to new profit paths for your business.

If you don't know where to start, try the professional membership group(s) for your business or primary target audience. Google any topic of interest and add "data" or "research" or "information" to see what you will find. Searching on Wikipedia could yield references to something or somewhere valuable.

- **Customers and Clients Are in Charge**
  Today, when people want to buy an appliance, visit a restaurant, hire a repair person or consultant, they do their homework first. Making cost comparisons, getting the facts

about how companies do business, and learning about others' experiences with that product or company are all part of "shopping." Once folks get a sense of how they feel about a business, product, or service offering, then they ask friends and family, before diving more deeply into reviews and opinions from strangers.

The statistics bear this out:

- 63% of consumers said they would give a brand preference if it provided interesting, relevant, or valuable content. Doing so increases credibility and, therefore, visibility in the marketplace. *Rapt Media*

- 48% of consumers use a search engine to begin mobile research, while 33% visit a site they already had in mind—and presumably use the content there to make their purchasing decisions. *Smart Insights*

- 73% of consumers say they are more likely to choose a product or service if they can learn more about it through a video first. Useful content doesn't have to be text-based. *Animoto*

- 88% of consumers who search for a local business by typing on a mobile device make contact by phone or in-person within 24 hours. This puts them just one step away from conversion. *Nectafy*

Actual point-of-sale contact happens last. Your company wants to grab attention before that point—before it's too late to sway opinion.

Benchmarking can help you present information on prices, business practices, and industry direction. Providing data-driven marketplace information positions your company as the credible, helpful authority in your domain.

Let's say that your benchmark study gets picked up by a major publication in your business sector, such as Inc Magazine, Forbes, or CIO Magazine. It might be posted in a large industry group on LinkedIn, or your leading professional organization.

The piece credits your organization, and suddenly, you've reached a much wider audience. You also gain from the prestige afforded those respected outlets. With one informational product, you've upped your company's credibility and visibility—just like that!

- **Information with Actionable Insights is the New Currency**

Consider how many other companies post interesting and relevant articles that relate to their brand expertise. A lot, right? So, let's focus on this qualifier: valuable, insightful, breakthrough material.

Gone are the days when the mere act of constantly pumping out general content gets attention and engagement. With so much research to do, customers want information that is directly useful to them. This could be numbers-oriented information like the previously noted stats on client or customer behavior that might be of value to your prospects. Or it could be trickle-down information based on data such as preferred customer products or factors that help businesses see where they fall in the competitive landscape.

> "Gone are the days when the mere act of constantly pumping out general content gets attention and engagement."

Benchmarking is a means of tracking and making the information relevant to your target online. When you do this, your content can attract new leads every time it's shared on LinkedIn, Twitter, Facebook, SlideShare, YouTube (if you made a short video about it), even Pinterest, or in conversations with colleagues, clients, and prospects.

You don't have to directly feed benchmark conclusions to businesses for them to be relevant. You can use your findings to make changes to your own products or procedures to lower costs or to better serve customers. Then you can extend your study by measuring the results of those changes you made.

If you want to market your benchmark to other companies, this ongoing data analysis will pay off well into the future. The greater your data set or number of replications of your information and data gathering over time, the more valuable the insights will be. You can find numerous ways to use an initial study as a springboard to analyses of distinct aspects of your benchmarking focus.

"The greater your data set or number of replications of your information and data gathering over time, the more valuable the insights will be."

Next, we'll look at the many ways you can create your own branded benchmarks.

Types of Branded Benchmarks

You can go in many directions if you want to create, mine or enhance information that's valuable—in ways that large or small businesses and Solonaires™ (our trademarked term for one-person businesses or solopreneurs) can leverage. These will help you punch far above your weight class, so to speak. You can begin with one of these ways:

- Curate and add value by summarizing data from research conducted by others.

- Audit your own files, website, social media analytics or work processes for valuable information that can be shared internally or publicly for improvements and decision-making. Look for the information that can help you generate ideas, save money, or create new revenue streams and channels.

- Track and be first to share—among your own community, however small—valuable information for your audience and prospects.

Large companies are running fast with big data generated and wielded for all kinds of reasons. Most of them have the human and financial resources to accomplish their information-driven internal, external, and marketplace goals to build and maintain competitive advantage.

However, our focus here is on the small to mid-sized businesses, including solopreneurs. In fact, the opportunity for a one-person business is limitless. Let's carve out several options you can explore from the range of possibilities.

"The objective of benchmarking is to find examples of superior performance and to understand the processes and practices driving that performance," according to Bain and Company.[3]

The tracking can be internal for an organization, external within an industry, or across industries. More on that is below.

> "The objective of benchmarking is to find examples of superior performance and to understand the processes and practices driving that performance."

Consider developing one or more of these five types of benchmarks that can offer value and help position your expertise, authority, and attract clients.

1. **Awards and Recognitions** – A recognition or award represents acknowledgement of a person, a group of people, like a sports team, or an organization for their excellence (or achievement) in a certain field. These can be based on data you track "in the wild,"—through your own research, based on specific criteria you establish, or through invitations for submissions based on determined sets of criteria.

   The recognition or award can then be leveraged toward yet another recognition perceived as equal or greater value. For example, REBRAND 100® Global Awards, provided information and criteria for the REBRAND Hall of Fame™.

   If the recognition and awards are conducted internally, they can provide a way to document, showcase and share preferred actions and behaviors within an organization. Similarly, a recognition or award outside the company, even held to acknowledge customers/clients or an outside organization, go a long way to seal their positive perception of your brand/company. It can also help you garner precious media attention.

   You already know that positive attention is a path you can lead to profits. Visibility that enhances credibility, trust, and authority is the lifeblood of a thriving business.

2. **Curated Reviews** – These can result from interviews, your own research, round-up of existing public information or your periodic predictions. Examples are "Best of..." or "Worst of ..."

3. **Industry Index** – In business, an index is a way of measuring and tracking change in a representative group of products, services, or even organizations. The index is calculated by averaging the quantities generated by individual components of the monitored group, thereby revealing the up or down movement in performance over a selected time period such as daily, weekly, or annual.

4. **Periodic Research and Surveys** – Research or surveys you conduct on your own or with a collaborator can yield useful, newsworthy results–all positioning you as an authority.

5. **Rankings and Lists** - A ranking is a presentation of items or individuals to show their relationship to each other based on an identified criteria. Rankings and listings typically reveal those relationships through an assessment of which component is higher or lower than the other. These can result from your own research, surveys, or from submissions you requested with a particular set of guidelines.

In creating and promoting your branded benchmark, we've found that having periodic consistence with schedule is important. For example, if you commit to doing something once a month, then do it. If once every two years, stick to that. If annual, keep it annual. Once folks are trained on when to expect your information, this helps boost reach and attention.

PART 2

“Set boundaries on your subject matter, your resources, and the procedure, and you’ll be set up for success.”

GETTING STARTED WITH BENCHMARKING

Now that you're aware of the value of your own distinct benchmark, keep your eyes open for white papers, reports, infographics, and even press releases that can serve as examples or sources of inspiration. Review some to see what is and isn't useful or compelling about them.

Your goal is to create or curate your own original, relevant benchmark. Then, set out to brand that benchmark.

Worthwhile information is out there for any business to take to market and monetize. And there are many ways to mine data. Do you want to put your brand on a study of repeat customers, or look at how clients chose your product or service? Do you want to find out how your business performance ranks against market leaders—and why? Or, can you find a new way to add value to someone else's existing research?

The first step is to look for information gaps that your ideal prospects want and need to be filled. In filling these gaps, your options include either internally or externally focused data collection methods.

Internally Focused Data Collection

This benchmarking approach is derived from available information that your company already has or can easily access.

What do you have on hand that you may be taking for granted? Perhaps an outsider (even a current client, customer, partner, or collaborator) can help you realize its value or quickly create something that would be marketable to them or others.

Consider:

- Tracking what you would like to improve
- Reviewing your own existing data and archives
- Enhancing or extrapolating existing measurements
- Partnering with local businesses, nonprofits, or industry groups in your sector
- For larger groups...implementing the NPS® (Net Promoter System®) for your organization and sharing what you learn from that in monitoring your organization's advocates, detractors, and passive audience, including their feedback on interactions with your company. You just need at least 20 respondents for the NPS to generate useful information.

> Note: NPS® or Net Promoter System® measures customer experience and predicts business growth.[4]

Externally Focused Methods

This means of formulating benchmarks might include:

- Quick surveys
- Live interviews
- Original research on a specific topic
- Review of research by others
- Round-up of existing data enhanced with insights
- Review of submissions you requested

How to Choose a Benchmark Focus

Narrow your focus—but not so much that it doesn't provide value. The problem with data is there is always more of it. When you select a single metric, you exclude others. If you group metrics, you may wind up with too much data to comprehensively address.

Benchmarking should not be an open-ended process. Set boundaries on your chosen subject matter, your resources, and the procedure and you'll be set up for success.

Going back to our example of ImpactValuator, one key finding of the database of the brand implementation benchmark can be distilled in the ratio, 1:20. This single data point is an essential one that an organization planning for brand change must know.

Before the ImpactValuator database was tracked and developed, companies were in the dark about the real costs of rebranding. But with that important insight, they can decide on how to phase the implementation of changes to fit with their budget and critical timelines. Without fail, whenever a compelling graphic is created with that ratio, it results in many shares and visits to the VIM Group website to learn more.

Explore Popular Topic Areas

Consider which information gleaned from your business experience will be useful for client prospects, customers or other companies. At the same time, think about how your business can gain from this knowledge as well.

For instance, suppose you create a study about customer reactions to telephone wait times on hold. You may plan to go public with a report, but you can also use your findings to adapt current practices to improve customer care in your business. Topics that have two-fold purposes reap double the rewards.

Review the Preferences of Your Ideal Client

Every business has clients who are critical to their revenue. Repeat customers, those who are loyal to a brand, and those who do not incur high costs for service or product delivery, are ideal. Bargain shoppers, indecisive shoppers, and those who take an inordinate share of employee time, complain often, or frequently request refunds, are less than ideal.

You, as well as the businesses that might see your presentation or report, want to increase the pool of ideal customers. So you may track what pleases your best audience. Is it reasonable pricing, convenient interactions, great client results, customer experience, unique products and services, or all combined?

You may already have these answers from periodic surveys, recorded phone calls, or customer testimonials. Or, you might have to gather this information through questionnaires or interviews.

Harvest Information Gaps

Your company may routinely conduct performance reviews that tell you much about how your business stacks up against the competition or how to build on its strengths. What haven't you explored in the past?

If you have identified but not acted upon weak spots in your company, build a benchmark study around those. What impact do those weaknesses have on your client base? How do other organizations address similar flaws? What are the consequences if they don't?

Other targets for missing information could include aspects of expansion, the choice to align with growing market trends, and new opportunities that might be within reach in the near future. Apply your company's experience with, or curiosity about, these potential business moves to the benchmarking process. Or, compare your track record with other companies' positive or negative outcomes.

How about research, a study, review, or survey using your skills and experience to develop valuable information for an industry that could use your expertise? For example, while there might be much available for consumer product brands, what about industries that are less "sexy" like utilities, oil and gas, or construction?

Ask Clients or Your Community What They Want to Know

If you're not sure which direction to take or what data might be of value to others, conduct a preliminary survey of what customers or existing clients would like to know. Just come right out and ask them. A custom-designed benchmark study can directly serve your client base, improve your

"A custom-designed benchmark study can directly serve your key client base" internal operations, or result in unique market intelligence that other businesses will pay for.

If you don't yet have clients from an audience you want, then research who does. You may discover that you can collaborate with them in a way that is mutually beneficial. If not, strive to reach those prospects on your own.

Keep Benchmarking Affordable

Surveys, database management, analysis, infographics, presentations, and design all cost time and money. How you carry out the benchmarking process can make or break your ability to fund it from start through completion. Like any kind of research, planning will keep the project on track, so it won't spiral out of control or drag on indefinitely. Besides curtailing the scope of benchmarking, you'll want to look at ways to keep costs down or share expenses through partnership and collaboration. This will reduce the impact on your bottom line while increasing reach down the road.

"Like any kind of research, planning will keep the project on track"

Start Small

The concept of benchmarking as a directly or indirectly profitable endeavor is exciting, but plan well. While planning, keep the big picture in mind as you decide how much you can realistically do. Just as there is always more behavior or action to track, there will always be more opportunities to curate or create benchmarks.

> "Be realistic in designing a benchmark study or original research"

Go ahead and think big, but start small. Be realistic in designing a benchmark study or original research, putting aside for later the things that you would like to do but that are outside of your current financial and logistical capabilities. For example, it would be nice to know how your telephone wait times compare with those of industry leaders, but you first need to find out how your current wait-time status affects your current customers or prospects.

Some social media platforms have polling tools to conduct a quick one- to three-question survey. If you are delivering a webinar, most webinar platforms have polling or survey features that can accomplish two things:

1. Increase engagement with your audience.

2. Generate useful data and insights you can share. If the number of respondents is significant, it is worthwhile to create an infographic around what you have learned and share it.

Choose a single metric to pursue—or a couple of closely related statistics. Maybe you will survey patient customers about the wait-time issue and be able to infer why you lost the impatient ones. Investigating how wait times affect purchasing behavior and how your sales performance ranks in the market sector can be the subject of your next study.

Stay Focused

The research obstacles may frustrate your team. Even a tight plan won't account for new insights that arise during the data collection or analysis process. Your team may come across opportunities to consider related information, such as how a call-back option might mitigate lost calls due to wait time. For example, instead of customers waiting on the phone, the company takes the callers' numbers, keeps track of their places in the queue, and calls them back.

Researchers recognize that intriguing threads, like this one, are temptations to go down a rabbit hole, chasing after information that may or may not serve the goal at hand. That doesn't mean you have to ignore new directions; just save them for later. Stay focused, and you'll be more likely to stay within budget and within schedule.

Cut Costs or Piggyback Information

Suppose you've decided on a one- or two-question customer survey to get your initial data pool. If you've planned to email a stand-alone questionnaire to your customer email list (if you have one), how could you reduce expenses?

You might embed two questions into your online checkout process and skip the email, for those buying something from you. Or, you could add the survey step to online customer service forms, live chats, telephone interactions, during a webinar you conduct, or via your social media polling tool.

Perhaps you want to analyze the social media usage of a particular group within an industry. Do you know of another business, other than a direct competitor, that might have the same intent? This could be a public relations firm or a social media consultant that could work with you.

Non-competing businesses may jump at the chance to partner on a benchmark project and share expenses. They may be interested in an executive summary later or purchase a more extensive report with findings and recommended actions to mitigate the problem. They can help you increase reach when promoting the benchmark, especially if it helps them promote their services. Remember, you have potential partners from industry associations, other businesses that offer complementary services, or others who might be able and willing to work with you. As noted, one benefit of tapping into a broader network also comes later, in extending your reach when the time comes to publicize and market your benchmark.

You can also cut costs on follow-up studies by simply pouring your original benchmark data into a new study that expands the sample size or focuses on a different aspect than your first analysis. Building on previous results is an ideal way to enhance your information pool because it reduces your expenses. At the same time, you increase the return on your investment. You can do this indefinitely.

Roadmap to a Successful Benchmark

Now that you have a clear direction and parameters, you can get ready to create a benchmark. To successfully complete the process, these guidelines will help:

- identify a valuable topic and a way to measure what you set out to assess
- review information or knowledge you already have or can easily track with a partner or resource
- design a process that will help you gather and sort the information you're tracking within your current resources (time, money, people, and partners)
- make your results digestible and relevant to your target audience
- present and promote the results in a compelling way with actionable insights

- anticipate questions your benchmark might inspire, and prepare answers for them (helpful for media outreach)
- evolve and consult with others who will boost awareness and offer feedback

Here are the steps you'll want to take, keeping the guidelines above in mind:

1. Define Your Why

What are your goals for establishing a benchmark? To generate leads? Increase conversions? Position your company, c-suite, or other key individuals as thought leaders on a particular subject? Who are you targetting?

Your goals will inform the rest of the benchmarking process. Clarifying them will also help keep you focused. With your main goals in mind, you can include or rule out options in your process.

For instance, if you want to generate leads, you'll want to measure data that's of immediate value to your defined ideal prospects. If you want to move to the forefront of your market sector, you'll want a broader range of data from outside sources that corroborate your findings, and then draw further conclusions from those. This could be a longer game than quick hits for a lead generation strategy.

2. Establish a Compelling Topic

Come up with several possible focus points for the benchmark study. Before you make your selection—and before you put time and money into it—get a sense of the reception your topic might receive.

> "Come up with several possible focus points for the benchmark study."

It's worthwhile to conduct some initial

research into your topic. Make sure your company has some expertise or a credible reason to be heard on the subject. Find similar studies, if any, for domain expertise, and determine how you can make yours unique enough to strongly differentiate and reflect your brand.

3. **Design a Methodology**
   Come up with a methodology that contributes to your overarching goal for the benchmark. This covers the combined steps of collecting, analyzing, and presenting the data with insights.

   Don't short-change the presentation part of the process. All the data and conclusions you generate will be useless if no one reads or benefits from the results. The same goes if nobody understands the information and knows what to do with it.

4. **Compile the Data**
   As you move through active data collection, remember to focus on your project goals. Stay on track and analyze the points that form your thesis. You will now arrive at the moment of truth: take the time to think through your findings and their implications. This is the catalyst for turning raw data into actionable insights.

"Be clear and concise in describing what you've studied and its value to them."

Before writing the summary report, consider your audience. Be clear and concise in describing what you've studied and its value to them. Ask yourself: What is the takeaway message? Why does it matter? Then give real-world examples that powerfully demonstrate the significance of the benchmark. Those examples could be from specific topics, companies or brands you encountered during your study. Once you have a valuable body of information, present it in a way that makes the greatest impact on your target audience. First, revise it to reflect or raise interest in your brand. Then, create a visual presentation that both draws viewers in and streamlines the reading experience. We'll delve more into graphic presentation in **Part 3** and brand elements in **Part 4**.

"Once you have a valuable body of information, present it in a way that makes the greatest impact on your target audience."

5. Summarize Your Results

Whether your branded benchmark report is short or long, you might use the information to improve your products, services, or company processes. The usefulness of your benchmark, however, may not be obvious to other end users. Don't be afraid to tell them. Be specific.

In the executive summary or benchmark report introduction, summarize the salient findings. "We learned... which means... which gives you...." When they realize the value of your findings, readers will want to know more.

Still, some may be too busy to get all the details. In that case, be ready to share your bullet point summary, infographic, report, summary presentation, via a recorded interview, podcast appearance, blog post, webinar, or slides. These highlights from your study are nuggets you can repurpose for other uses such as quotes, social media updates, or video clips on your home page. You can even trademark phrases and link them to your brand.

6. Partner, Promote and Market

You'll need to promote your branded benchmark and see that it reaches its intended audience. If you have collaborated with partners, they will help to promote your findings. This is crucial for getting maximum value for your company or organization.

Brand positioning is key. That's why an entire section of this book is devoted to strategies for that in **Part 4**. Your company can use a well-received benchmark report as a news item or a calling card to solicit business from a new audience or market.

7. Follow Up, Evolve, and Extend

Follow up on reactions to your results and use these to help you design future studies. You can leverage your branded benchmark to approach influencers and opinion leaders in your industry and ask them for their opinion on your findings—letting them know that you may include them in your marketing and promotional plans, of course. Many would appreciate being quoted in something that promises to be important in the industry, if properly and professionally cited.

Iterate your survey or study based on previous results and responses. Your market or subject matter will also evolve, which can prompt an evolution in your own branded benchmark or the methodology you use.

Finally, you may want to consider extending your benchmark. This might mean finding ways to make it more comprehensive, more useful to other stakeholders in your industry, or more applicable.

The bottom line is that your branded benchmark is not set in stone. You can—and should—always improve it.

PART 3

> “Anyone could track the same information, but they wouldn’t do it the same way you would for your specific industry and focus.”

MARKET YOUR BRANDED BENCHMARK

After creating your own benchmark, your work is only half-done. The other half involves getting it into the hands of those who will use it and spreading the word about it.

Much of the work you did earlier will help you promote and market your benchmark. If you partnered with another business to either generate or enhance the data, or if you tapped the resources of an organization for the data, then they can help you in marketing it and increasing reach through their networks.

Identify the unique angle of your benchmark: what sets it apart from competitors? The benchmark itself can be unique, or it can be for a new demographic or audience. If you used existing data, the angle could be the unique spin you've put on it. Anyone could track the same information, but they wouldn't do it the same way you would for your specific industry and focus.

Infuse it with insights and value that only those with whom you want to deepen a business relationship or attract, would appreciate. These are only some of the ways to differentiate your benchmark in a radical and meaningful way.

Naming and Positioning

An important task is to determine the name and positioning of your benchmark. Coming up with a name or title for your benchmark may seem like a trivial thing. However, keep in mind that this will create the first, and potentially lasting, impression among the benchmark's possible users. It helps determine whether your audience will pay attention to the benchmark, find it trustworthy, credible, and memorable.

We'll go deeper into this in **Part 4**, Brand Positioning.

Create a Microsite for the Branded Benchmark

Consider creating a basic website for your benchmark. The website will become the anchor of your benchmark's online presence. It can be a one-page site with the highlights of your benchmark and links to download the full report. If you repeat the study over time, subsequent reports can be available on the site.

"Even if you're using the benchmark to build your email contact list, make a version of it available for free"

Even if you're using the benchmark to build your email contact list, make a version of it available for free, without requiring sign-up. You'll find that people are more likely to share links to your research if it's on a page that's not "gated." That is, it doesn't require people to sign up in order to access. Examples of ways to make your benchmark freely accessible include: a blog post summarizing the main findings, an infographic that's free for anyone to share with proper attribution to you, and a video of the highlights.

Special Note: Importance of Privacy

If you provide copies of your report in exchange for a person's contact information (such as their email address), make sure you adhere to General Data Protection Regulation [GDPR], Controlling the Assault of Non-Solicited Pornography and Marketing [CAN-SPAM] Act, and Canada's Anti-Spam Legislation [CASL], depending on which laws apply to you. GDPR applies to the European Union, CAN-SPAM to the United States, and CASL to Canada.

This refers to the location of those that engage with where you operate. If you're based in the United States but have email subscribers in France, for example, your business needs to comply with GDPR. You must check on privacy regulations of any location where your current or prospective customers might reside. In general, respect for and proper stewardship of individuals' identifiable information is key.

Package the Benchmark

You'll want your benchmark to be compelling, digestible, handy, and shareable. To achieve all this, You'll need to package and present your benchmark in different formats and media to help achieve those goals. Remember that visuals attract attention and have more viral potential than plain text.

- Prepare the full report for those who want to dive into the details. Decide if you want to give away the highlights but sell the full report.

- Create an executive summary. Quick to disseminate and grasp, an executive summary raises interest in your benchmark.

- Publish a blog post or article on your website to announce the completion of the benchmark and share some findings. If you're tracking the same benchmark over a long period, you can identify trends discovered from year to year.

- Brainstorm headlines that you'll use on everything from web pages and email subject lines, to social media posts and video titles. Compelling names and headlines grab attention.

- Deliver the benchmark highlights into formats, such as:

    - **Infographics** – Make sure it tells a coherent story. Don't just slap statistics on an image and call it a day. Inform relevant blogs and organizations about the availability of your infographics.

    - **Slide decks** – You can use this to present the benchmark to various groups. Share it on SlideShare (slideshare.net), linking to or embedded at your website and/or the benchmark microsite. Encourage others to embed the slides on their website to increase exposure.

    - **Video** – Video content now dominates the web. Create a video based on the executive summary, telling the story of the insight data, index, or your other benchmark type. And then create one video block for each key finding. Keep videos short and inviting. A video can be the recording of Powerpoint or Keynote slides with short text overlays.

> You might also record the slides with a voice over (yours or someone you designate). Describe the few highlighted slides—say 10 or fewer.

As you leverage and repurpose the benchmark for various platforms, be careful that you don't contribute to the content clutter. Whatever you put out there needs to tell a story. Pull out a few salient points or main take-aways. Pick out something strong and bold. You don't have to share everything when you're trying to entice people to then look for more. Remember VIM Group's ImpactValuator? Its single most compelling datapoint is a simple ratio, 1:20.

That's all it takes to start engaging with people. Then, if they want more, you can provide more details when they show interest by reaching out to you.

The Importance of Design

Design is such a crucial element of positioning and marketing your branded benchmark that it deserves its own section. Design the report to align with your brand and enhance the communication of the key findings. When you create the look and feel for the benchmark, aim for simplicity, clarity, and distinct visual impact.

Use a coherent design in all materials pertaining to the benchmark, both online and offline. There are many examples of large and small companies sharing results of their original or enhanced research. Let those you discover inspire you.

Promote on Social Media

Social media marketing is the easiest way to promote your benchmark. Beware of spreading yourself too thin, since you have limited time and resources. Define a social media strategy and implement it. Focus your efforts on one or two social media platforms where your target audience is most active. Be sure your profiles on these platforms are updated.

Next, create attractive and compelling, visually-impactful posts for these platforms and schedule them to be shared over days, weeks, or months, making sure the information is timely and relevant. Monitor your accounts and respond whenever somebody engages with those posts, whether by posting a comment, liking, or sharing. Take note of which individuals and groups show the greatest interest and follow up with them to keep the conversation going, if appropriate.

It also helps to have content for different platforms, including the ones you aren't active on. For example, even if you don't plan to be active on Pinterest, make sure images are "pinnable" by those who share their finds on Pinterest.

Harness the Power of Public Relations

PR is alive and well, so don't overlook this powerful tool. Create a PR plan, no matter how simple. Traditional media may be hungry for news about your benchmark. Laura Kane, former Chief Communications Officer of the Public Relations Society of America, has been quoted as saying,

> "It is easy for journalists to find people who are willing to share an opinion on a subject, it is rarer to find someone who has data points related to that topic. Original research and related data makes you a credible source for reporters and can help you develop a following of interested stakeholders."

Get your branded benchmark ready for media exposure:

Media Kit

Make it easy for media to pick up on your benchmark. A kit of materials they can use, both for offline and online relevance, will help. Publish a digital version of your media kit on a PR resources page at your existing website, or on your benchmark microsite, if you have one.

Your kit can be develop over time to include:

- Press releases – Write a press release on various stages of your benchmarking process, not just to announce your findings. Even before the benchmark is complete, you can raise anticipation for it by publicizing the initiative. Every time you present the benchmark in an event (in-person or virtual), create a press release about that as well. Then add to your media kit or media page.

- Fact sheets – A fact sheet is an at-a-glance view of the most important information about your benchmark. This is the quickest summary you can offer a prospect to save them the trouble of going through your entire website, or reading through reams of other information. You can create a single fact sheet or separate fact sheets for the methodology, key findings, and use cases of the benchmark.

- Images – Provide copyright-free images that content publishers can use when speaking or writing about your benchmark, or indicate how the ones without copyright clearance should be credited.

- Profiles/Bios – Include profiles (short bios and downloadable photos) and contact information of the leadership behind the benchmark as well as spokespersons on the topic.

- Videos – On your printed media kit, include a link to the videos you created for your benchmark. On your web-based, digital media kit, embed the videos directly on the media resources page. Allow others to embed the videos as well on their websites or social media channels. Include embedding tips for them.

- Quotes – Formulate your own “quotable quotes” from the benchmark study and disseminate them in different formats. They can be text, graphics, video, and/or audio sound bites.

- Social Media Updates - Provide sample tweets or posts with impact along with images, especially for social platforms where your audience is most active.

- SlideShare – Create a slide deck with highlights of the benchmark. Upload to slideshare.net (accounts are free) and embed on your media resources page.

- Press Write-Ups/Interviews - Be sure to gather press write-ups with links, interviews, recorded webinars, recorded podcasts, social media mentions, and add to your media kit or online resources page.

Events

Launch your benchmark through an event, whether in-person or virtual. For instance, you could organize a press launch for local media (if applicable), during which you announce your key findings. If this sounds too intimidating, consider launching your benchmark through online live streaming. If you have a strong and engaged community on Facebook or YouTube, a live video stream on either of those platforms is a virtual event that can get the attention of your intended audience.

Facebook has a live video feature, and Google Hangout was the tool for creating instant videos on YouTube. You can also use platforms like Zoom or Go To Webinar to deliver live information in real-time.

For those with an up-to-date email list, or collaborators with large audiences, a webinar is another type of virtual event that can get you publicity, both in traditional and new media.

Whichever type of event you create to launch and present your benchmark, here's an extended list of ideas to repurpose your benchmark and the results:

1. Upload the recording(s) as a video on YouTube to help position yourself as an expert. Break these up into bite-sized lengths for easier, convenient consumption by your viewers.

2. Transcribe the video and include the text in a PDF you sell or give away as a guide. Or break it up into shorter reports and publish as a blog post or social media updates.

3. Survey or poll your audience, during a webinar, for example, and turn the results into yet another report.

4. Expand on the findings and turn the insights and recommended actions into an online or offline course you teach or have someone else deliver.

5. Break up, sell, or give away the presentation with recordings of audio modules of each.

6. Use each section (if you can get up to three or more) for downloadable study materials you send weekly

via email for a three weeks+ course for attendees. Then follow up with once-a-week live calls when you can have real-time dialogue with students.

7. Embed the audio/webinar/SlideShare presentation and give it away on your website to direct traffic to your site.
8. Use pieces of content for your newsletter or emails.
9. Edit the presentation/report and add introductory content that specifically addresses various niche markets and sell them separately. This is only if the benchmark is relevant for various industries.
10. Use the content in blog posts, Twitter posts, LinkedIn articles, or updates on your Facebook or Instagram.
11. Use the materials—slides and outlines—to give a talk in person, and distribute the outline as a bonus handout.
12. Use the material to develop a checklist or worksheet.
13. Use the material to develop a step-by-step workbook.
14. Use the material in your own book or grant permission for inclusion in someone else's book.
15. Use the material to run a live workshop/strategy session for an organization, if applicable.
16. Excerpt or expand the presentation references as a resource list published as a bonus for attendees.
17. Develop a coaching or consulting service based on knowledge you gained.

Networking

Be ready to spread the word about your benchmark at networking and industry events. Always have a copy of the executive summary and other content pieces that may be of interest.

Your benchmark is also an opportunity for you to collaborate with leaders in your industry. Send them your key findings and ask for their reactions. Then, ask for permission to quote them when you promote the benchmark. Even the busiest experts are willing to give their two-cents on research in exchange for the exposure. In turn, they're more likely to tell other people about your research.

"Always have a copy of the executive summary and other content pieces that may be of interest."

Reach out to your existing network and look for opportunities to talk about your benchmark. These opportunities include guest-posting, podcast interviews, in-person meet-ups, and the like. Every time you address a new audience, find an angle of the benchmark that's appropriate for them.

Reach out as well to people you've hired for consulting or freelance services. Because you're a client, they're more likely to promote you to their audiences and connections. After all, you have invested in them and their services.

Printed Pieces

The old-fashioned printed piece still works and can be incredibly attention-getting. Mail a copy of the report or executive summary to prospects and clients. Make it an option for website visitors to request a hard copy instead of or in addition to a digital format. You can also approach your connections, such as on LinkedIn, to ask if they would like a copy mailed to them.

“Pay attention to packaging, because it can mean the difference between a piece that's opened enthusiastically and one that ends up in the garbage bin.”

Pay attention to packaging, because it can mean the difference between a piece that's opened enthusiastically and one that ends up in the garbage bin. How about using a clear envelope, so the recipient knows right away that the content isn't junk mail? Magazines often send their publications this way.

You might even send a larger sized postcard, say 6x9 or larger, with a great graphic of the most compelling finding on the front, next to the address field, and a few quick notes and stats on the back of that postcard. You could include a quick, hand-written note inviting the recipient to learn more from you with a phone call, by attending a meeting or joining a webinar.

Please note that these should be reserved for your most important and serious prospects. Packaging and postage expenses can be significant over time.

Market Through Amazon

Amazon is often neglected as a promotional platform. Upload your benchmark report on the Kindle Digital Publishing platform as a digital or printed book. As of this writing, Amazon's minimum requirements are 24 pages for a bound book and 116 pages for a printed book if you want to have a spine that contains words.

This helps because, as a published author on the world's largest online marketplace, you're entitled to have an Author Page. You can link this page to your website so that it shows your most recent blog posts.

Both your Amazon Author Page and book listings are crawled by Google and appear on Google search results. Since Amazon is a high-authority website—meaning it is trusted by Google for reliable content—these pages will likely rank higher for search results than your own website.

“Key components of positioning a benchmark include a specific audience, memorable name, clear distinction, tone of voice, and relevance.”

BRAND POSITIONING

Even before you share the results of your benchmarking efforts, you can begin to drum up interest through brand positioning.

Positioning is the process of differentiating your offer for clear strategic advantage in the minds of those you want to care and to choose you. It's your strategy for driving your competitive advantage.

Without brand positioning, your benchmark remains ambiguous and not instantly recognizable. It can disappear or gain little reach and traction. With careful planning and your initial steps of defining your why, establishing a compelling topic, and more, clues are evident on how to stake out a marketplace position for your branded benchmark.

Here are just a few benefits of strong, well-positioned brands:

- Most memorable name recall
- Drive marketplace value
- Establish authentic reputation and authority
- Build trust and loyalty
- Command a premium price
- Highly engaged employees
- Magnet for best employee talent
- Associated with quality
- Recover from reputational risk faster
- Attract partners, collaborators and investors

Key components of positioning a benchmark brand include specific group(s) you target, memorable name, clear distinction, tone of voice, and relevance. If the benchmark topic is valuable, those elements will help it reach more far and wide. These essential attributes must be integrated with a design, communications and marketing strategy.

Brand positioning matters because cutting through the content clutter to garner attention doesn't just demand distinction. It requires radical differentiation—what renowned branding expert, Marty Neumeier, suggests with "When others Zig, you ZAG!"

Brand Consistency vs. Coherence

Your company's brand may already have an established look and feel. If you are happy with it, then be sure to include pertinent elements of your existing brand in your benchmark positioning, so it aligns with your brand. If you are not happy with it, however, this may be the time to make bold and effective changes.

> "Key components of positioning a benchmark include... a clear audience, memorable name, clear distinction, tone of voice, and relevance."

You're going for brand coherence, not brand consistency. The brand elements, such as design of your benchmark, do not have to be identical to all that you apply for your organization. However, all elements and touchpoints should be noticeably part of an over-arching whole. Everything should convey one brand personality and experience. In this digital age, this means you have to be flexible enough to adjust to fit various touchpoints, and the corresponding physical and digital expereinces.

Mobile Matters

Since many access websites, apps, and digital products from their smartphones rather than their laptops or desktop computer, present your benchmark in formats that are mobile friendly. Doing so may mean that you break consistency with how you might present to those viewing from a computer or those you present to in person.

Naming

What you call something is essential. In fact, the name of a product, service, object—anything—is one of the most critical decisions you make. Unfortunately, many use generic words for their information, data, or research, missing the opportunity to establish something memorable and indelible in the minds of their audience.

A memorable and distinct name can become a shortcut for the information you are conveying. If you try your best to come up with a remarkable name, you will increase your chances of establishing your credibility, relevance, and attention. These are elements that ultimately help you convert more of your audience to paying clients.

"If you generate and publish your benchmark regularly, its name and/or tagline will become a shortcut that helps it grow with familiarity over time."

The benchmark name can also include a positive descriptor or tagline. This can be a short, memorable phrase that summarizes or describes the value of the benchmark. If you generate and publish your benchmark regularly, its name and/or tagline will become a shortcut that helps it grow with familiarity over time.

To get started with brainstorming names for your benchmark, consider answering the following questions suggested by Tori Miner, former Verbal Identity Director at Interbrand.[5]

- What is this thing?
- Who cares about it?

- Where will the name be in the market?
- How will people see and interact with the name?
- What do you want this name to say?
- How will it fit with other names in your portfolio?

> "A name should address both heart and mind: it should convey the heart of your brand, while remaining aligned to your business goals."

Miner further suggests that a name should address both heart and mind: it should convey the heart of your brand, while remaining aligned to your business goals.

Explore a few possibilities and conduct naming research before zeroing in on a single name. As is often the case, searching via Google or other search engines is a place to start. Naming research goes beyond asking your audience which name they prefer. It also includes observing how they respond to various names and how each name might be received in different cultures if your branded benchmark has an international, non-English-speaking target audience.

If you plan to create a microsite for your branded benchmark, you will need to register a domain name. Find one that's easy to remember that can be easily associated with your benchmark.

In his book, *The Brand Gap*, Marty Neumeier proposes seven criteria for a brand name.[6] We highly recommend this book.

1. **Distinctiveness.** Does it stand out from the crowd, especially from other names in its category? Does it separate well from ordinary text and speech? *Good rule: Give it the unique "presence" of a proper noun.*

2. **Brevity.** Is it short enough to be easily recalled and used? Will it resist being shortened to a nickname? Long multi-word names will be quickly shortened to non-communicating initials. *Good rule: No names more than four syllables.*

3. **Appropriateness.** Is there a reasonable fit with the purpose and value proposition of the entity? Can it cross cultural boundaries without negative consequences? *Good rule: If it would work just as well—or better—for another brand, keep looking.*

4. **Easy spelling and pronunciation.** Will most people be able to spell the name after hearing it spoken? Will they be able to pronounce it after seeing it written? *Good rule: A name shouldn't turn into a spelling test or make people feel ignorant.*

5. **Likability.** Will people enjoy using it? Names that are intellectually stimulating, or provide good "mouth feel," have a headstart over those that don't. *Good rule: Look for names that are "chewy" or "catchy" so that they stick. "Safe" or bland names tend to slide off.*

6. **Extendibility.** Does it have creative "legs"? Does it lend itself to a visual representation? Great names provide endless opportunities for brandplay. *Good rule: Choose a name that triggers mental images.*

7. **Protectability.** Can it be trademarked? Is it available as a URL? While many names can be trademarked, some are more defensible than others, making them safer and more valuable than others. *Good rule: Be different (see rule #1).*

Finally, remember that the name is only one element of building your powerful, branded benchmark. However, it is an important one that should not be left as an afterthought.

Onlyness

Your goal with a strongly branded positioning for your benchmark is to be in your own defendable category of ONE. This is another excellent concept that Marty Neumeier elaborates on in his books and workshops. For a brand to be well-positioned in the marketplace, it is essential to determine and summarize the unique, compelling benefit your benchmark provides. Therefore, you must clarify and communicate your benchmark's Onlyness (sometimes written as Onliness).

If you are the ONLY one at something that is relevant, valuable, and compelling to your market, then you don't compete! As Marty Neumeier noted,

> "Onliness is by far the most powerful test of a strategic position. Brands need strong positioning because customers [and clients] have choices—if you don't stand out, you lose.
>
> Discover what makes you the only, which is nothing less than a journey to the core of your business.[7]"

With effective positioning, even if copycats come along and do something similar, your benchmark would already be entrenched as "first" in people's minds:

When "first" is done well, you begin to build trust, credibility, familiarity, before those copycats. There's more to brand positioning. However, if you apply the tips we offer here you'll be far ahead of many.

In business, positioning has a geometric, not linear, effect on market share. This also applies to benchmark brand positioning. The benchmark that establishes itself as number one in its category will have double (if not more) the share of audience compared to the second benchmark, and so on.

"In business, positioning has a geometric, not linear, effect on market share."

Onlyness Exercise and Examples

One way to establish the Onlyness for your benchmark is to apply Neumeier's Onlyness Exercise. Complete the following statement.[8]

Our (offering) ______________________________

Is the ONLY (category) ______________________________

That (benefit) ______________________________

Tip: Your benchmark should either solve a problem, fill a missing data gap, fulfill a desire, reveal, clarify, or recommend a process.

It's best to keep your Onlyness statement to 12-15 words maximum. If you can make it shorter, even better. A little longer is okay. Just be as concise and compelling as possible.

Note: We highly recommend purchasing, Marty Neumeier books which you can find on Amazon.com and visiting his website martyneumeier.com

Examples of branded benchmark Onlyness statements:

BUILDPLAY Digital Index™ is the **ONLY** digital performance **Index** that tracks A/E/C brands.

ARCHITECT 50 is the **ONLY** annual US **ranking** of firms based on business, sustainability, and design performance.

Interbrand's **Best Global Brands** is the first and **ONLY** annual brand valuation **ranking** of global brands.

The **REBRAND 100® Global Awards** is the **ONLY** juried global **recognition** for effective brand transformations.

Examples outside the realm of benchmarks:

MOVEO is the **ONLY** lightweight electric scooter that folds up for easy storage.

ASSET Framework is the **ONLY** new profit path roadmap for A/E/C brands.

Amy's Drive Thru is the **ONLY** fast food restaurant that sells organic food.

Twitter is the **ONLY** social media platform with 280-character messages.

When coming up with your benchmark's brand positioning, aim for memorable, compelling, original, relevant, well-designed, and newsworthy.

Visual Identity

"Strong visual design with relevant images, bold, clear colors and graphics are essential to brand positioning."

You can harness the power of strong, simple, confident design with visuals to get attention. The human mind is hard-wired to see what's different. Just imagine: If you have a bowl of green apples with one single red apple, your eye immediately sees (and more easily remembers) the lone red apple. Strong visual design with relevant images, bold, clear colors and graphics are essential to brand positioning.

Your benchmark can have its own, distinct look, but remember to strive for coherence. It should still visually align with the overall look and feel of your business or organization.

Here are some examples of the visual identities of branded benchmarks as of this writing:

BUILDPLAY Digital Index™

World Architecture 100

Prophet Brand Relevance Index

REBRAND 100® Global Awards

Interbrand Best Global Brands

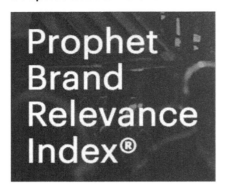

When you choose a name and create a visual identity for your benchmark, consider having it trademarked. You're in this for the long haul and you want the name, logo, and slogan or tagline (if you have one) protected against being used by somebody else. Eventually, all this will become part of the brand of your business. You wouldn't want to be doing all this work only to build brand awareness for another company.

"When you choose a name and create a visual identity for your benchmark, consider having it trademarked."

Hopefully you have learned much from this guide. Not only have you learned how to create your own branded benchmark, you might also consider guiding others through the process.

Later, you could offer services to prospects on ways to design and create their own study or develop a benchmark for them. By doing so, you will enable them to achieve powerful results with this type of valuable, original research that could help them accomplish their business goals.

PART 5

“Your goal with strongly branded positioning for your benchmark is to be in your own defendable category of ONE.”

CASE EXAMPLES OF BRANDED BENCHMARKS:

- Awards and Recognitions
- Curated Reviews
- Industry Index
- Periodic Research and Surveys
- Rankings and Lists

These case examples are compiled to inspire and motivate you with what's possible. These depictions are as of this writing.

We encourage you to visit the links to the benchmarks to track their updates. Consider going on your own benchmark treasure hunt and jot down what you find on the pages provided for your notes, at the back of the book.

1. ABI - Architecture Billings Index

Benchmark Type

Industry Index, Periodic Research and Surveys

Owner/Proponent

American Institute of Architects (AIA) - aia.org

Description

The Architecture Billings Index (ABI) is a diffusion index derived from the monthly Work-on-the-Boards survey conducted by the AIA Economics & Market Research Group. It's an economic indicator that leads nonresidential construction activity by approximately 9-12 months.

Methodology

AIA's survey panel asks participants whether their billings increased, decreased, or stayed the same in the month that just ended. Depending on the proportion of respondents choosing each option, a score is generated, which represents the month's index value.

An index score of 50 represents no change in firm billings from the previous month, a score above 50 indicates an increase in firm billings from the previous month, and a score below 50 indicates a decline in firm billings from the previous month.

Users

International investment groups, major media, small firms, real estate developers and business leaders in the A/E/C —–architecture/engineering/construction—space

Use Cases/Examples

ABI helps industry members and leaders assess business conditions. It also helps firms prepare for market fluctuations, plan resources, establish hiring and managing budgets, and make decisions around finding client leads.

Reporting

ABI is published every month and distributed to subscribers and AIA members. Each month's report is published on a page at AIA's website and can be downloaded as a PDF.

Summary findings for each month are communicated in one image such as this one from March 2020.

It represents the extent to which billings and design contracts have changed from the previous month.

The rest of the monthly report breaks down the survey findings by region and sector. The report also includes a write-up with an analysis of the findings, insights from the survey results, and selected quotes from respondents.

Promotion

ABI is often quoted in industry publications, such as ARCHITECT Magazine and Archinect. Anyone interested can subscribe to receive ABI by email every month.

More Information

bit.ly/2HmCkAt

2. Big Mac Index

Benchmark Type

Industry Index

Owner/Proponent

The Economist

Description

The Big Mac index, also known as the Big Mac PPP, is a light-hearted measurement of whether currencies are at their "correct" level. It is based on the purchasing power parity (PPP) theory that exchange rates should move towards the rate that would equalize the prices of identical goods and services (in this case, a burger).

Methodology

The Big Mac PPP exchange rate between two countries is obtained by dividing the price of a Big Mac in one country (in its currency) by the price of a Big Mac in another country (in its currency). This value is then compared with the actual exchange rate. If it is lower, then the first currency is under-valued compared with the second. Conversely, if it is higher, then the first currency is over-valued.

Users

Schools and universities, economists, media, researchers

Use Cases/Examples

Aside from explaining the concept of PPP in layman's terms, the Big Mac Index has become a global standard for gauging currency misalignment. According to The Economist, it has been included in several economics textbooks and is the subject of at least 20 academic studies.

Reporting

The Economist publishes the Big Mac Index through an interactive currency-comparison tool on its website. Users can choose between five base currencies—yuan, euro, yen, pound sterling, and US dollar—and click on a map to see whether a country currency is under- or over-valued.

The full data set is also downloadable at no cost in Excel format from the website.

Promotion

The Economist announces the results of each year's Big Mac Index. It is also reported by various economics- and finance-oriented media.

More Information

econ.st/2LjhjfK

3. BUILDPLAY Digital Index™

Benchmark Type

Curated Review, Industry Index,
Periodic Research and Surveys

Owner/Proponent

BUILDPLAY™ (Part of the REBRAND Alliance)

Description

BUILDPLAY Digital Index is the first digital presence review study for the A/E/C (architecture, engineering, and construction) industry, conducted by BUILDPLAY™, a global platform that tracks digital and brand profiles of A/E/C firms.

Methodology

The study covers the top 50 of the top 100 architectural firms ranked in BDOnline magazine's annual World Architecture 100. Each company's website and social media usage is reviewed with an emphasis on LinkedIn—the leading business-focused platform. What's checked includes whether their websites are mobile responsive and secure, which social platforms are integrated, the company LinkedIn profile and corresponding posts and updates.

The first BUILDPLAY Digital Index, using quantitative and qualitative measures was conducted in 2016. The graphic below depicts a portion of the 2019 study.

BUILDPLAY Digital Index™

The BUILDPLAY Digital Index is the first digital performance study for the A/E/C (Architecture/Engineering/Construction) industry. It tracks information on websites and social media platforms and analyzes data with a focus on Linkedin, the foremost B2B social media platform.

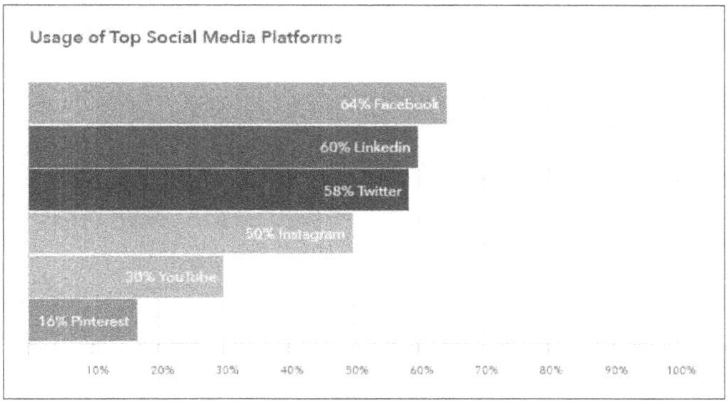

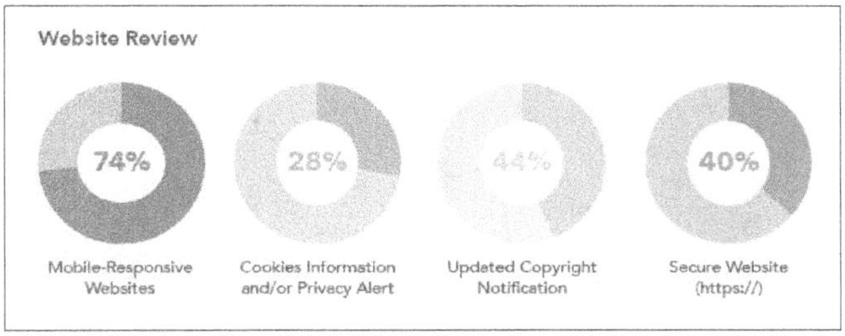

Users

Architects, real estate developers, commercial property managers, interior designers, engineers, construction firms/ builders, marketers, investors, employee/talent prospects, and others involved in the built environment industries.

Use Cases/Examples

The AEC industry lags behind many others in the use of social media, especially the very essential LinkedIn for B2B companies. This benchmark helps industry players improve their websites and optimize their social media presence.

It will also help firms integrate Google's required features for websites to be properly ranked and found through search. The summary report is complemented with insights and tips on how to improve reach and results.

Reporting

BUILDPLAY Digital Index results are shared in live and online presentations and through social media. A PDF of results is freely available, without needing to submit contact information, at BUILDPLAY.com/index.

Promotion

Aside from live presentations and webinars, findings are promoted through social media (particularly through ArchitectureBiz on Twitter), direct email to A/E/C groups such as American Institute of Architects (AIA) and SMPS (Society for Marketing Professional Services).

More Information

buildplay.com/

4. Edelman Trust Barometer

Benchmark Type

Periodic Research and Surveys

Proponent

Edelman

Description

The Edelman Trust Barometer is an annual survey by Edelman Intelligence, a global insights and analytics consultancy, and a division of Edelman PR. It determines how much people all over the world trust business, government, NGOs, and media.

Methodology

The Barometer is based on an online survey in 27 markets with over 33,000 respondents. In developed countries, respondents are made up of a nationally-representative online sample that closely reflects the general population. In countries where internet usage is low, the respondents are more the affluent, educated, and urban segment of the broader population.

Users

Politicians, institutions, businesses, academics, and media find the Trust Barometer useful for various reasons, including how to navigate the volatile state of trust/distrust in order to achieve their communication and general goals.

Use Cases/Examples

The report provides rich fodder for commentaries about various institutions. Opinion makers use it to prescribe ways for members of specific industries to increase trust and gain credibility. For example, based on the 2018 Edelman Trust Barometer, Ron Carucci wrote the article, “How to Build Trust When Working Across Borders,” for Harvard Business Review.

Reporting

The latest findings are published at the Edelman website (edelman.com/trust-barometer), along with editorial pieces about the results.

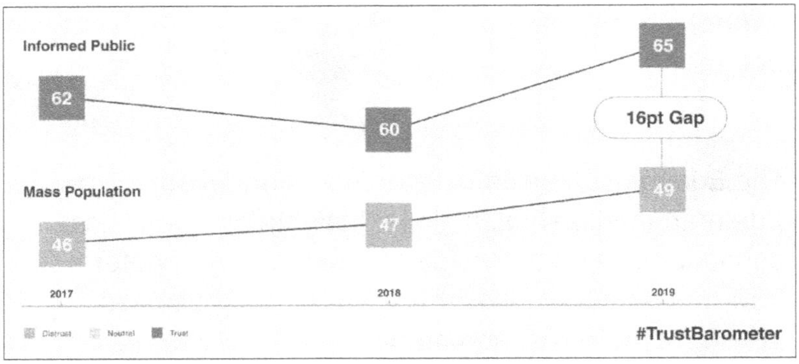

An executive summary is provided that breaks down results by country, region, and institution types. The executive summary and global results are available as downloadable PDFs. That summary compares trust levels between the general population and the informed public (educated, higher income individuals).

Promotion

Trust Barometer results are promoted through PR and social media, such as YouTube videos.

More Information

edelman.com/trust-barometer

5. Fast Company Innovation by Design Awards

Benchmark Type

Awards and Recognition

Proponent

Fast Company & Inc, Mansueto Ventures LLC

Description

The annual Innovation by Design Awards is a competition that honors creative work in design, business, and innovation. The goal of the awards is to highlight the best design work from freelancers, startups, and multinational corporations.

Now beyond its seventh year, previous awardees have included blue-chip companies, startups, and young talents. It is one of the most sought-after design awards in the industry and draws thousands of submissions every year.

The judges include designers from a variety of disciplines, business leaders from some of the most innovative companies in the world, and Fast Company's own editors.

Methodology

The competition is open to all organizations and individuals involved in designing a product or service that was made public or came to market within a specific time period.

Over 30 judges rate entries on the key ingredients of innovation: functionality, originality, beauty, sustainability, user insight, cultural impact, and business impact. Winners are selected in 15 categories, which range from apps, to places, to user experience.

Users

Designers, businesses, innovators, marketers, researchers, educators, PR professionals

Use Cases/Examples

Winners and finalists use the recognition in their marketing and promotions. Other designers and businesses gain inspiration from winning designs.

Reporting and Promotion

Winners, finalists, and honorable mentions are featured online and in the October issue of Fast Company magazine. Winners are also celebrated at Fast Company's Innovation Festival in the fall.

Fashion and Beauty

Ministry of Supply's Voice-Enabled, Intelligent Heated Jacket
Ministry of Supply

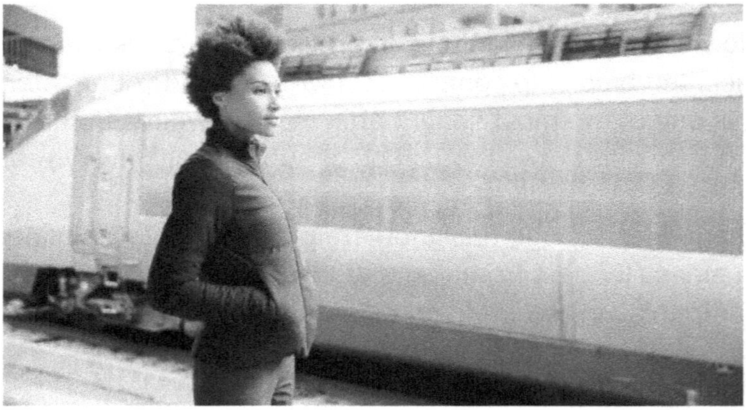

Gihan Amarasiriwardena, Co-founder and President, Ministry of Supply; Aman Advani, Co-founder and CEO, Ministry of Supply; Luke Mooney and Jean-Francois Duval, Co-founders Dephy (Boston-based human robotics company)

More Information

bit.ly/33iHokz

6. Interbrand Best Global Brands

Benchmark Type

Periodic Research and Surveys, Rankings and Lists

Proponent

Interbrand

Description

Best Global Brands, an annual report which began in 1999, analyzes the marketplace value of global brands. According to the Interbrand website, the study shows "how brands grow in a changing world, showing that using technology at scale to deliver intimate human experiences, will help drive economic growth value."

It also ranks brands by region (e.g., Best Asia Brands), by specific country (e.g., Best Brazilian Brands), and by industry (e.g., Best Pharma Brands). Businesses and investors can certainly apply the insights gleaned in many ways.

Methodology

To be included in Best Global Brands, a brand must be global, visible, growing, and relatively transparent with financial results. Using a wide range of information sources, each brand is ranked on three key components:

- financial performance
- influence on customer choice
- ability to command premium price or secure earnings

The rankings for these key components make up each brand's cumulative value. This methodology has been ISO certified (International Organization for Standardization), the first brand valuation method to do so.

Users

C-suite of brands, brand managers and consultants, marketers, business researchers and professionals.

Use Cases/Examples

Best Global Brands can be a strategic tool for brand management and those who wish to better understand it. With its rich and insightful analyses, the report paints a clear picture of how each brand is contributing to business growth and how the brand can deliver even greater growth. Brand valuation is also useful when assessing brand strategy and investment options.

Reporting

The report has dedicated pages at the Interbrand website. It includes the latest and previous findings broken down by geographical location and industries.

There is a page for each brand, which includes interactive charts and brand-specific data. The full report can be downloaded for free as a PDF, after submitting your contact information.

Promotion

Interbrand promotes Best Global Brands through PR, related articles on its website, and social media. The brands included in the study also publicize their inclusion on the Best Global Brands list.

More Information

bit.ly/2YO6V5O

7. Landor M&A Brand Study

Benchmark Type

Curated Reviews, Periodic Research and Surveys, Rankings and Lists

Proponent

Landor

Description

The Landor M&A Brand Study, released in 2017, is the first in-depth quantitative analysis of merger and acquisition (M&A) branding activity. It provides an objective benchmark on the relationship between acquisitions and brand change.

The study also includes a database with information on sector- and company-specific brand transition factors during acquisitions including target geography, strategic rationale, size and type of deal, number of acquisitions made, and the timeline involved.

It is a definitive benchmark of M&A activity and its impact on brands and brand integrations of S&P 100 companies across different industries. Some of the brands included are Alphabet, Apple, Chevron, Dow Chemical, JPMorgan Chase GE, PepsiCo, Pfizer, Procter & Gamble, Texas Instruments, Visa, Vodafone and Microsoft.

Methodology

Landor leveraged machine learning to analyze the M&A behavior of S&P 100 companies over the past 10 years. They analyzed 2,300 acquisitions and 120,000 sources of unstructured data, such as press releases, web documents, financial statements, and investor presentations to learn when, why, and how acquired brands are rebranded.

Users

C-suite leaders, corporate strategists, M&A advisors, brand consultants and investors, researchers.

Use Cases/Examples

Louis Sciullo, Executive Director of Financial Services at Landor, who led the study said it best: "It can help them see how competitors in their sector—and companies in other industries—have handled M&A, and which strategies have resulted in successful acquisitions. To maximize value for companies during an M&A, it's important that brand strategy be an ingredient throughout the deal process—not an afterthought."

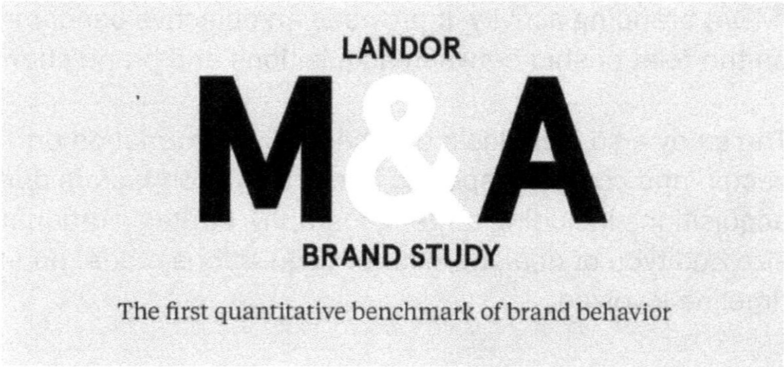

Reporting

The Landor M&A Brand Study findings are available on the Landor website. The study infographic, which summarizes the key findings, is also available for free download.

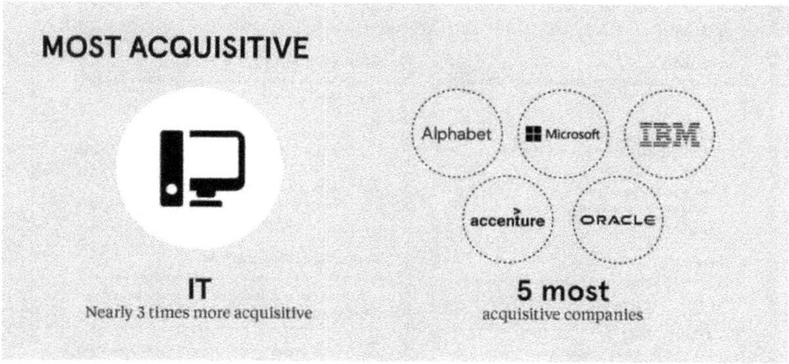

Promotion

The study and its findings have been reported by various business and marketing-oriented publications and websites. Sciullo has given a number of interviews to promote the results and to discuss their implications for brands.

More Information

bit.ly/2ze1Y6I

8. Mijks Digital Airport Index

Benchmark Type

Index, Periodic Research and Surveys, Rankings and Lists

Proponent

Mijksenaar

Description

The Digital Airport Index assesses the maturity level of digital integration at airports. Mijksenaar's goal is to create seamless experiences for passengers at airports worldwide.

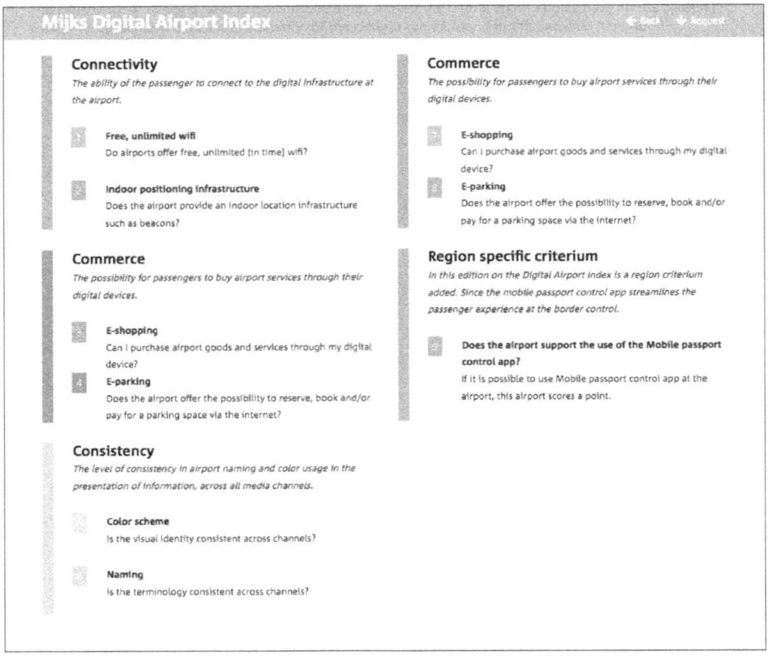

Methodology

The Index assesses, compares, and rates the digital customer journey in four areas: connectivity, communication, consistency and commerce. When the index was first launched in 2017, it covered 50 European airports. Since then, it has expanded to include North America, Latin America, Asia, Africa, and Oceania.

Users

Airport managers, travelers, travel agencies, airport vendors, travel industry professionals, and anyone else who spends time in airports

Use Cases/Examples

The results are used by airports as a basis for improving and promoting their facilities. Some high-ranking airports have been using the Index in their marketing and PR.

Reporting

The Index is published by region (e.g., North America, Latin America, Europe) and is available on the Mijksenaar website. PDFs of specific regional indices are available for those who want more detailed information.

The information is organized in a table format for each airport in the region with a summary at the top. Criteria for measuring the digital performance of the airports are included at the website.

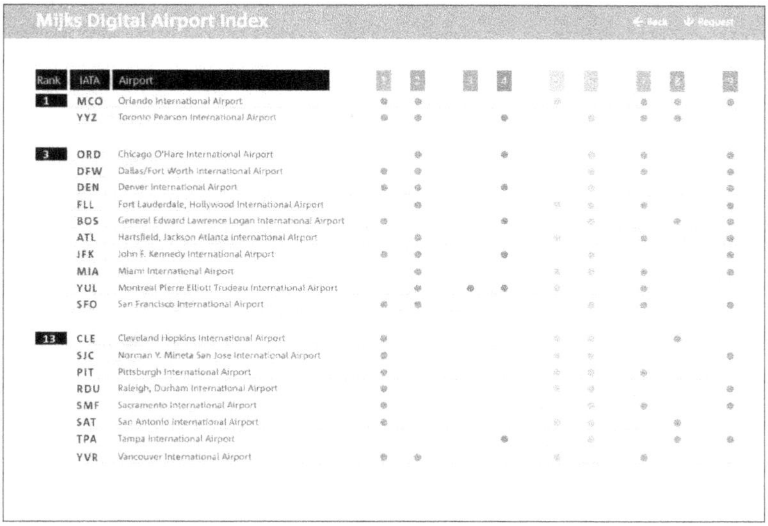

Promotion

Mijks Digital Airport Index is promoted via social media and through industry contacts. There's a microsite displaying the results of each region's index.

More Information

dai.mijksenaar.com/

9. Prophet Brand Relevance Index®

Benchmark Type

Industry Index, Periodic Research and Surveys

Proponent

Prophet

Description

Consulting company, Prophet, believes that the strongest brands are relentlessly relevant and make a difference in consumers' lives. The goal of the research is to understand the principles that great brands execute against—in customers' minds—in order to establish themselves as relentlessly relevant.

Methodology

Prophet surveys 50,000 consumers in China, Germany, United Kingdom, and United States to determine which 750 unique brands, including 150 global brands and 600 regional brands, they simply cannot live without.

The companies are selected from all industries that contribute materially to household spending. Smaller companies that have been driving change in these industries have also been included if they have demonstrated significant traction with consumers.

Not all brands in every category are included. Brands in the tobacco and firearms categories and companies engaged solely or primarily in business-to-business (B2B) categories were not included.

Users

Companies, brand experts, academic institutions, investors journalists, educators, businesses, researchers

Use Cases/Examples

The Prophet Brand Relevance Index helps business and brand leaders measure the relevance of their brand and find ways to improve it.

Reporting

The Index includes reports from the US, UK, Germany, and China, available in PDF in English, German, and Chinese. Each report opens with the criteria that the Index applies and a breakdown of the top 50 brands in the region.

A section notes the key findings and an analysis of consumer demographics for each country. For example, here's an image from their 2019 US Report:

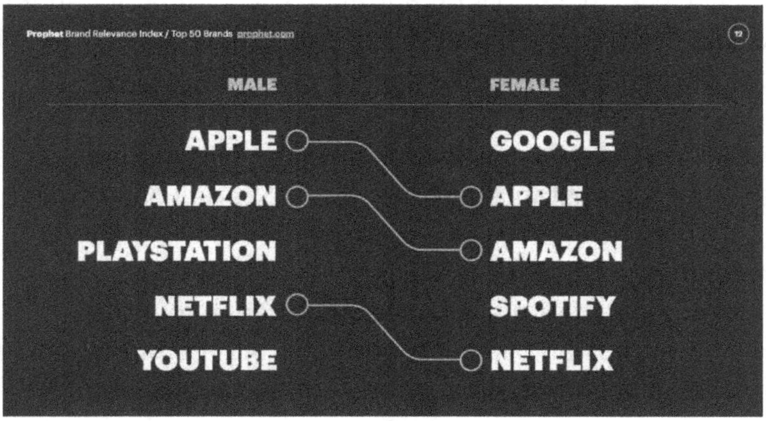

The rest of the report includes details about the top 50 relevant brands in the region.

Promotion

The index is promoted through social media, PR, and resources at a dedicated section of the Prophet website. The Index has also been featured in articles in publications like Marketwired and Forbes.

More Information

bit.ly/2YrKPXC

10. REBRAND 100® Global Awards

Benchmark Type

Awards and Recognitions, Curated Reviews, Rankings and Lists

Proponent

REBRAND™

Description

The REBRAND 100 Global Awards assess the effectiveness of brand transformations from around the world in various industries. The program launched as an annual event in 2004. It is currently held every two years. A total of 63 countries have participated in the awards, as of this writing. Businesses, non-profit organizations, government entities, brand owners, consultants, and agencies from anywhere in the world can enter.

REBRAND 100 Global Awards provided information that led to criteria for establishing the REBRAND Hall of Fame™.

Methodology

A new panel of jurors is convened for each round to review entries and select winners. Jurors are prominent, multidisciplinary leaders, representing various countries. Companies, organizations, or agencies can submit entries. Eligibility is for enterprise-wide transformations, change in a brand component, or an extension from an existing brand.

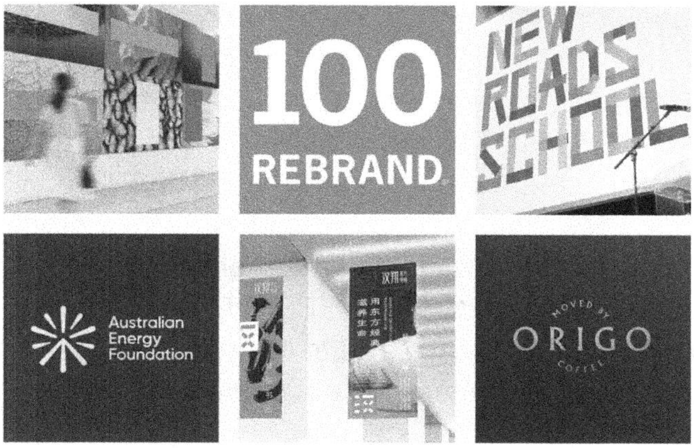

Jurors review entries within a two-week window and identify global, regional, and small brands as the winners over three main categories of winners: Five Best of Awards, Distinction, and Merit.

Users

Winners, researchers, educators, academia, marketers in general, business educators, brand agencies, consultants, business strategists and organizations looking to rebrand use the showcase pages for learning and inspiration.

Use Cases/Examples

Ashland, a global specialty chemicals company that was a past Winner of Distinction of REBRAND 100, created a section on their website to tout their winning strategy, tied to their repositioning as a problem solver.

Reporting

Winners are announced on the REBRAND.com website. Each winner is showcased on a dedicated, full page on the site. Some entries include a video or audio file in addition to the standard slide show with before and after examples. A project summary of 300 words or fewer is also required.

Some past winners have included brands like HP, Coty, The Country of Bhutan, Fiji Airways, Cancer UK, Audi, Siemens.

Promotion

REBRAND announces results to the winners and the public through press releases, traditional media outreach and social media. The winners themselves promote the, results through their own PR efforts. REBRAND provides press release templates, visual elements, and other assets that winners can use to publicize their win. Brands and consultants can invest with REBRAND to help support their efforts to increase reach and to leverage the positive news about their win. Winners are also widely promoted on social media with a dedicated, followed hashtag.

More Information

rebrand.com

11. Simplicity Index

Benchmark Type

Industry Index, Periodic Research and Surveys
Rankings and Lists

Proponent

Siegel+Gale

Description

First conducted in 2010, the Siegel+Gale Global Brand Simplicity Index is an annual rating of global brands on their simplicity and how they make people's lives simpler.
It generates two scores: An Industry Simplicity Score™ and a Brand Simplicity Score™.

Methodology

Siegel+Gale conducts an online survey of 14,000+ consumers in nine countries who rate over 850 brands on their perceived simplicity and how industries and brands make people's lives simpler or more complex.

Respondents rate each industry on whether it makes life simpler or more complex, the quality of typical interactions with companies in the industry, and how the industry's communications rank in terms of understanding, transparency/honesty, concern for customers, innovation/freshness, and usefulness.

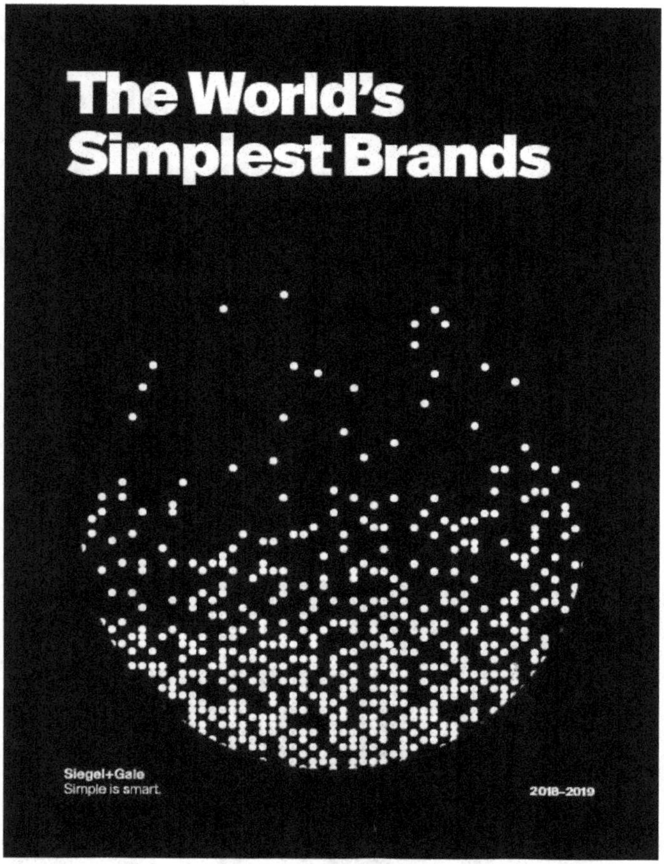

Each brand is evaluated on the simplicity/complexity of its products, services, interactions, and communications in relation to industry peers. The score factors in the consistency of responses, the difference between user and non-user perceptions, and the simplicity score for the brand's industry.

Users

Business consultants, brand managers, designers, investors, marketers, researchers, management consultants

Use Cases/Examples

Researchers, brands and industries that want to make the customer experience more user-friendly

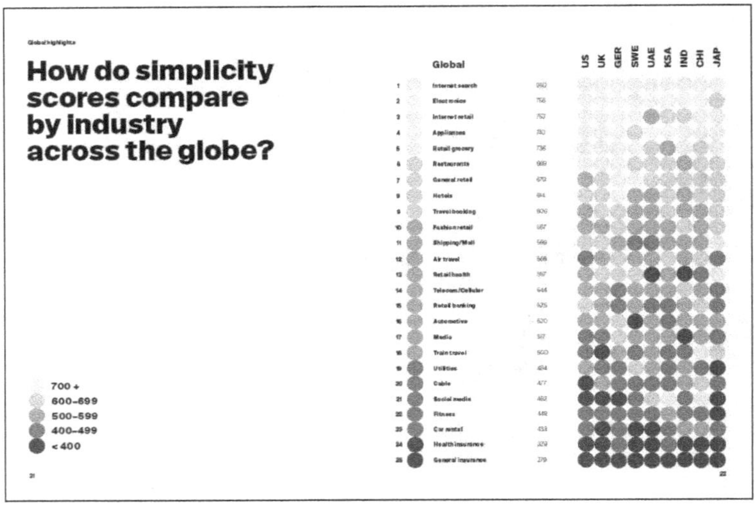

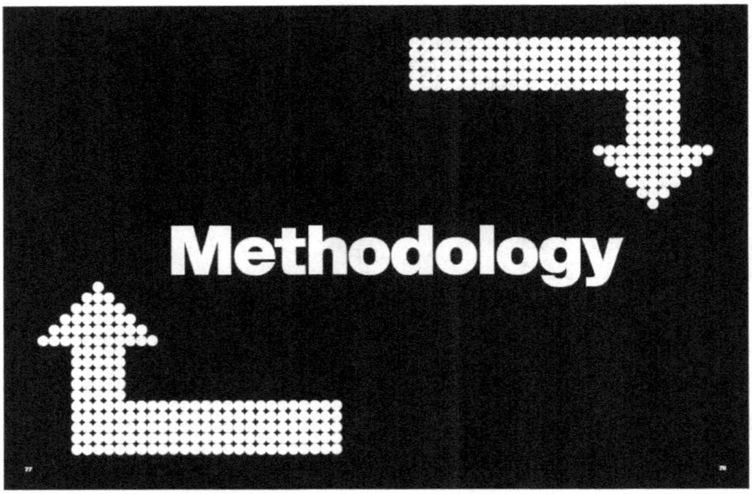

Reporting

The annual index is reported on the Siegel+Gale website and its own microsite, simplicityindex.com. A full report for the latest year's data can be downloaded through the site. Overviews are available as well, either globally or for the following regions: United States, United Kingdom, Germany, Sweden, China, Middle East, India, and Japan.

The brands from each region can be sorted in various ways, such as Top 10, industry, country.

Promotion

The Simplicity Index has been featured in numerous business publications such as Forbes and the Harvard Business Review. Anyone can download a copy of the report after submitting contact information on the Simplicity Index website. Siegel+Gale also shares results at social media channels like Twitter, Facebook, LinkedIn, and Instagram.

More Information

simplicityindex.com

12. T+L Top 500

Benchmark Type

Periodic Research and Surveys, Rankings and Lists

Proponent

Travel + Leisure Magazine

Description

T+L Top 500 is an annual rating of the top hotels, resorts, cities, islands, cruise ships, spas, airlines, and other travel and leisure-oriented businesses.

Methodology

The editors of Travel + Leisure, in association with research firm M&RR, developed the survey with respondents made up of readers of Travel + Leisure magazine, T+L tablet editions, newsletters, social media, and travelandleisure.com.

They rate hotel brands and other leisure activities on a number of characteristics: rooms/facilities, location, service, food, and value. For each characteristic, respondents choose a rating of excellent, above average, average, below average, or poor. The final scores are indexed averages of these responses and become the basis for the rankings in any of the World's Best lists.

Users

Travelers, hotels, resorts, and other travel-related businesses such as travel/tour organizers, journalists, marketers of travel-oriented products and services.

Use Cases/Examples

Travelers consult the T+L World's Best Awards to select destinations, hotels, and activities for their trips and vacations. Travel and leisure brands use the results to improve their products and services.

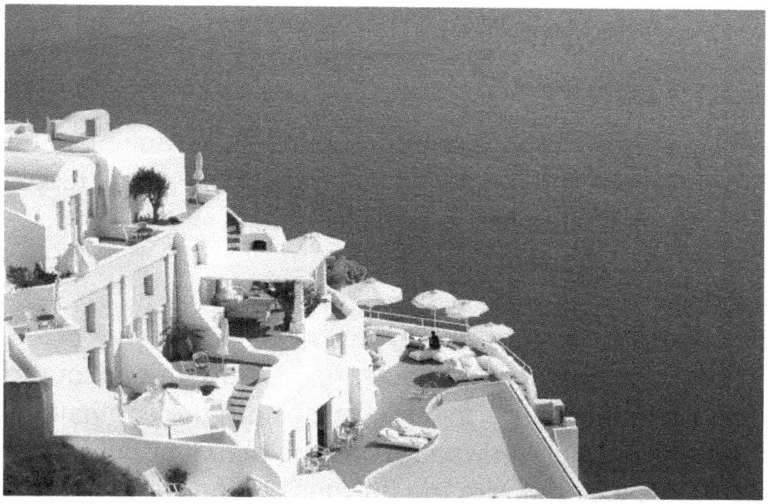

Courtesy of Katikies Hotel

Reporting

The annual World's Best Awards are reported on the Travel+Leisure magazine at travelandleisure.com. The list itself is presented in an article format, where the ranking counts down from 100 to 1. The average rating of each hotel is stated to two decimal places, and the website of the hotel or hotel brand is linked at the bottom for more information.

Promotion

Travel + Leisure promotes the survey findings to all its readers and social media audiences. Brands that make the Awards use it to promote their services.

More Information

travelandleisure.com/

13. TeenBusiness® Top 20

Benchmark Type

Curated Reviews, Rankings and Lists

Proponent

TeenBusiness Media™

Description

TeenBusiness® Top 20 entrepreneurs is the ranking of teen entrepreneurs and innovators compiled from global research and articles posted at the website.

Methodology

The criteria for making the list includes one or more of the following: the actual or potential positive impact of the business or innovative thinking on society, the originality of the business or innovation, and the actual or potential revenue associated with the business or innovation.

Users

Media, small businesses, teen business owners, entrepreneurs, educators, parents, investors

Use Cases/Examples

TeenBusiness highlights the incredible innovations, businesses, breakthroughs led by teenagers for purpose-driven and sustainable profit. It also provides useful information for educators, parents, mentors of teen businesses entrepreneurs, and potential investors,

Reporting

TeenBusiness Top 20 is published and distributed through press releases, showcase media highlights and social media posts. Winners are featured and showcased at the website video. A downloadable PDF is also available at the TeenBusiness website.

Promotion

TeenBusiness Top 20 is shared and re-shared primarily via social media. The winners help to extend the reach and media touchpoints by announcing their inclusion on the list to their network.

More Information

teenbusiness.com

14. The State of Fashion

Benchmark Type

Industry Index, Periodic Research and Surveys

Proponent

Business of Fashion + McKinsey

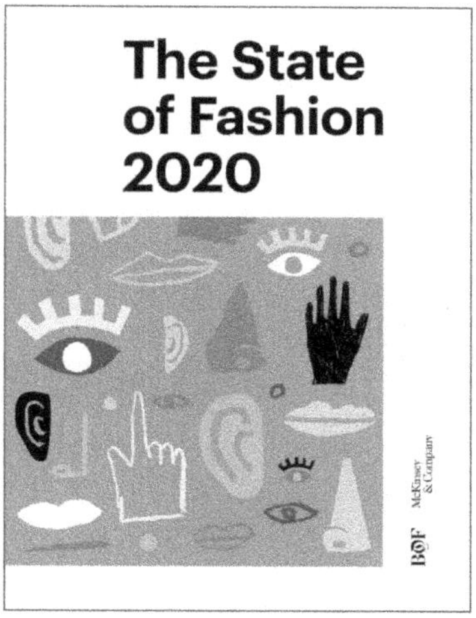

Description

The State of Fashion report provides a comprehensive view of the fashion industry, summarizing its current and projected performance and addressing the factors that shape and drive the industry. It shows the interconnectedness of the entire fashion ecosystem across regions, market segments, and product categories.

The report includes the McKinsey Global Fashion Index (MGFI), which analyzes and compares how a fashion company is performing against others in its market segment, product category, and region. The index also tracks industry sales, operating profit, and economic profit (value creation).

Methodology

The report uses extensive qualitative and quantitative analyses, drawing on industry and proprietary sources, including interviews of over 200 senior industry executives around the world and some of the most influential and forward-thinking people in the industry. The index covers over 500 retailers around the globe.

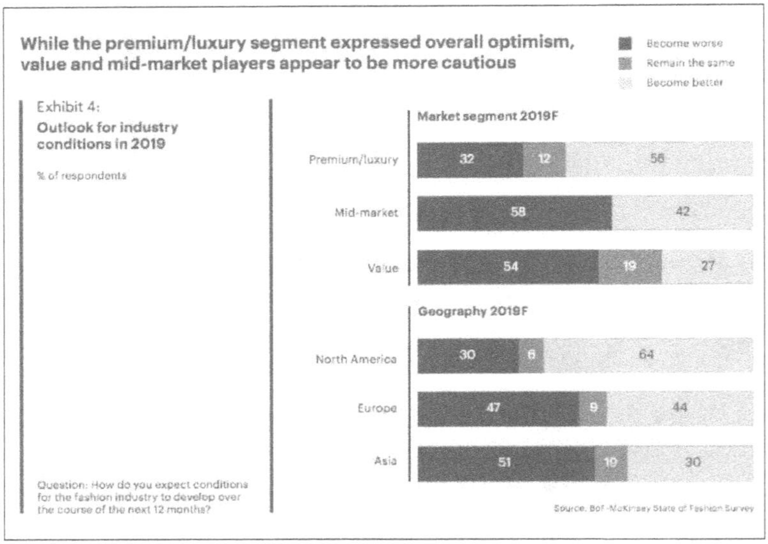

Users

The report can be used by anyone engaged in the business of fashion, whether as an entrepreneur, designer, investor or even as an informed shopper.

Use Cases/Examples

Industry leaders and related professionals can use The State of Fashion to determine their agenda for the coming year.

Reporting and Promotion

McKinsey publishes the main findings on their website and provides a downloadable PDF. Both organizations promote through social media and their PR and extensive offline and online channels.

More Information

mck.co/2VSPqOf

15. Twiplomacy

Benchmark Type

Curated Reviews, Periodic Research and Surveys, Rankings and Lists

Proponent

Burson-Marsteller

Description

Twiplomacy refers to the use of social networks by governments, inter-governmental organizations, and diplomats. The Twiplomacy study looks at how world leaders use social media, ranking them based on their influence, followers, interactions, and activity levels.

Methodology

Burson-Marsteller identifies the Twitter accounts of heads of state and government, foreign ministers, and institutions in 178 countries worldwide. They then analyze each leader's Twitter profile, tweet history, and connections.

Data is collected using Burson-Marsteller's proprietary Burson Tools to analyze over 700,000 possible Twitter connections between world leaders. Using crowdtangle.com, they capture the historic data for all accounts over the past 12 months.

Users

Researchers, politicians, educators, other leaders, journalists, government professionals, publications

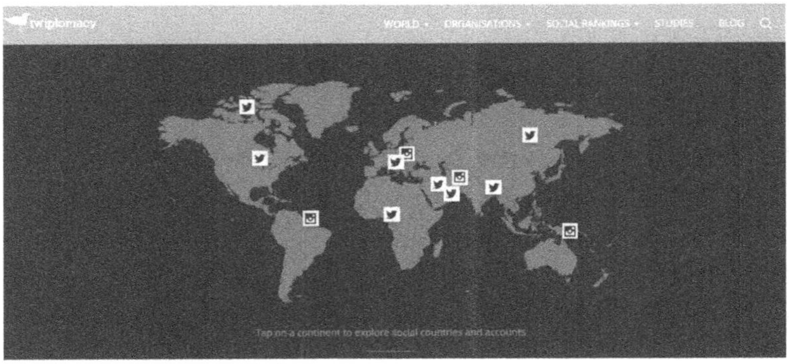

Use Cases/Examples

World leaders and organizations can use the findings to manage their social media strategies and activities.

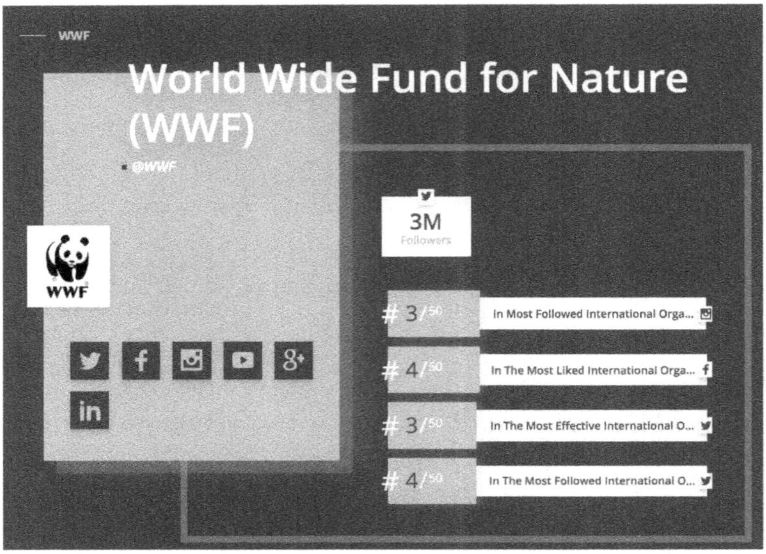

Reporting

The latest findings of the Twiplomacy study are published on a microsite, Twiplomacy.com. Results can be viewed by geographical location, organization, or social rankings (e.g., 50 Most Influential World Leaders, 50 Most Active World Leaders). The master data file can also be downloaded from the site in Microsoft Excel format.

Promotion

Twiplomacy study results are widely reported in both online and offline media outlets.

More Information

twiplomacy.com/

16. VIM Group ImpactValuator™

Benchmark Type

Industry Index, Periodic Research and Surveys

Proponent

VIM Group

Description

ImpactValuator is a study of the total costs of implementing brand change. Most companies anticipate only the cost of conceptualizing the rebrand, but not the impact of changing all physical and digital brand identity touchpoints to reflect the new brand.

ImpactValuator identified agency-to-implementation spend is 1:20. This means that the investment to implement brand change is typically 20 times the investment in brand consultants engaged for strategy and design to create the rebranding. They have found this index to have 85% accuracy, and a great gauge of the budget required.

ImpactValuator has also revealed that the average rebranding investment per employee over the last five years is $943 and rebranding costs amount to 0.5% of the annual turnover of international companies.

Methodology

VIM Group began computing the ImpactValuator index by tracking their work for over 1,200 brands since 2002. It also takes into account the industry of a brand, revenues, and number of employees.

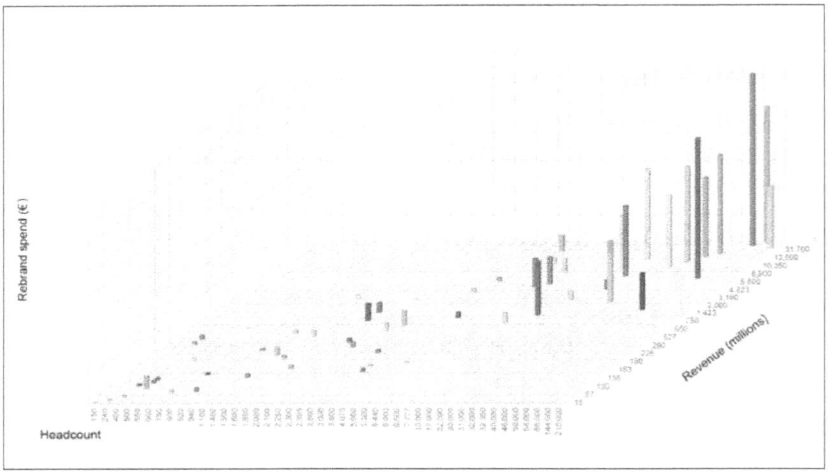

Users

C-suite leaders, companies planning to rebrand, brand consultants, vendors, investors, M&A professionals, marketers and educators

Use Cases/Examples

Using ImpactValuator, companies can more accurately estimate the cost and time frame that rebranding will require. Without the index, they run the risk of factoring in only the costs of the positioning and creative work behind rebranding. When the time comes to roll it out, they find themselves making concessions because they underestimated the full investment required to implement, and manage the brand assets.

Reporting

ImpactValuator was first reported on the VIM Group website. It is now made available during consultations and project engagement with clients.

Promotion

VIM Group's CEO, Marc Cloosterman, has written about ImpactValuator in blog posts and in articles on LinkedIn. Various branding-related websites and social media channels share the 1:20 data point, garnering much interest with each share. It has also been featured in the book, *Future-Proof Your Brand: Data-Driven Insights to Implement, Manage, and Optimise Your Brand Performance*, by Cloosterman and Laurens Hoekstra, VIM Group CSO.

More Information

vim-group.com/en/

17. World Architecture 100

Benchmark Type

Periodic Research and Surveys, Rankings and Lists

Proponent

Building Design (BD) Magazine

Description

World Architecture 100 is a survey and ranking of the world's largest architectural practices, ranked by the number of fee-earning architects employed by each firm. After being reported annually for over 25 years, it is now considered the who's who of international architecture firms.

Methodology

Each year, the survey is sent to over 1,250 practices worldwide. The resulting report covers three sections: Top 100 Chart (the top 100 practices are listed and ranked by the number of architects they employ), WA100 Profiles (a closer look at individual practices and their activity over the past year), and Market Sectors (the top leading practices in 15 sectors, ranked by fee income).

Users

Architecture firms, architects, engineering firms, real estate professionals, construction companies, industry leaders, influencers, investors, management consultants

Use Cases/Examples

Practices that make the list use it in their marketing. BD's own writers use the ranking as a take-off point to tackle various issues. Examples of these are articles like "What global architects think of Brexit."

Others use it to make observations about the industry. For example, Dezeen magazine used the 2017 World Architecture 100 results as the basis for its own research on gender diversity among the C-suite of top architecture firms.

Reporting

The summary list is published on bdonline.co.uk. Details are accessible only to registered users or subscribers. Digital copies of the full report must be purchased at bdonline.co.uk/wa-100/home.

WA100 2019

Rank 2019	Rank 2018	New	Practice name	Country	Architects employed	Fee Income (US $Million)
1	1		Gensler	USA	2627	
2	2		Nikken Sekkei	Japan	1869	
3	3		AECOM	USA	1733	$600-699m
4	4		HDR	USA	1491	$370-379m
5	5		Perkins+Will	USA	1148	$390-395m
6		New	Sweco	Sweden	1100	
7	6		IBI GROUP	Canada	862	$230-239m
8	7		HOK	USA	811	$290-299m
9	10		Aedas	China	761	$220-229m
10	8		DP Architects	Singapore	727	

Promotion

Results are reported by BD Magazine, architecture and design news portals, as well as by the firms themselves.

More Information

bdonline.co.uk/wa-100

18. World Value Index

Benchmark Type

Industry Index, Periodic Research and Surveys, Rankings and Lists

Proponent

enso

Description

The World Value Index measures how much Americans are inspired by the mission of brands. It also estimates the degree to which that inspiration translates into tangible support and purchases.

Methodology

This survey, which began in 2016, looks at four dimensions to measure a brand's Value Index:

- Awareness - respondent's awareness of the brand's purpose or mission beyond making money
- Alignment - whether the brand's purpose or mission aligns with what the respondent cares about
- Support - whether the respondent would openly support the brand's purpose
- Purchase – whether the brand's purpose or mission motivates the respondent to buy products or services from the brand

The study covers 200 brands, including for-profits, nonprofits, and social movements that have come to be identified as brands (e.g., Black Lives Matter, #MeToo, Women's March, etc.). Since 2018, the survey has also included individuals like Jeff Bezos, Rihanna, and the Pope.

The survey analyzes results by demographic and psychographic segments. It also looks at whether identification with class, race and gender are factors affecting success in America ('Class Aware', 'Race Aware', and 'Gender Aware'). As such, the study shows the relationships different audience segments have with brands.

Users

Brands, brand managers and consultants, investors, anybody interested in building and sustaining a mission-driven, purpose-oriented business

Use Cases/Examples

The study provides a better understanding of the role of mission and purpose on value creation. It's valuable to any mission-driven organization that wants to create more value. It can also shed light on the business opportunity of leading more strongly with values, mission, and purpose.

Reporting

The current year's main results are posted on a dedicated page on the enso website. It shows only the list of the top 50 brands by value, without details on each brand.

The full summary can be downloaded for free as a PDF after submitting contact details.

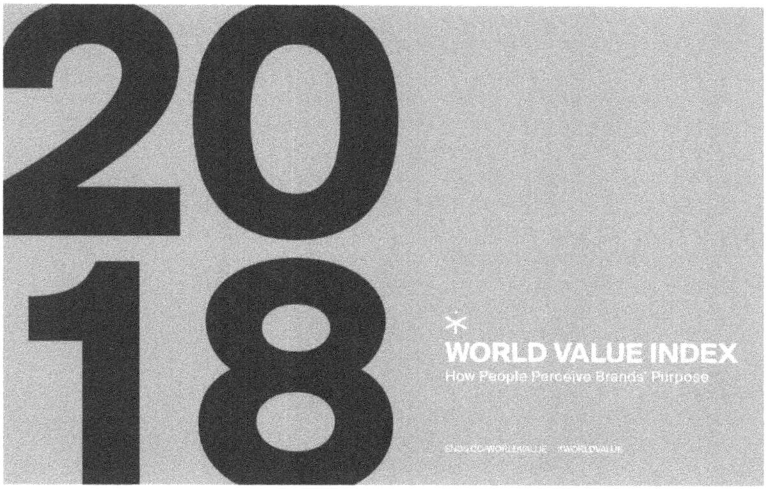

the 2018 World Value℠ Index

1. St. Jude Children's Research Hospital
2. Red Cross
3. Salvation Army
4. Goodwill
5. Habitat for Humanity
6. Doctors Without Borders
7. Amazon
8. Boys and Girls Club
9. Save the Children
10. Girl Scouts of the USA
11. World Wildlife Fund
12. Google
13. National Geographic
14. YMCA
15. Johnson & Johnson
16. Olympics
17. Campbell's Soup
18. Dove
19. Netflix
20. Disney
21. FedEx
22. Microsoft
23. UPS
24. Wikipedia
25. Samsung
26. PayPal
27. United Way
28. Kellogg's
29. Bill & Melinda Gates Foundation
30. YouTube
31. Nestlé
32. AAA
33. Kraft
34. CVS Pharmacy
35. Lipton
36. Home Depot
37. Walmart
38. Subway
39. Coca-Cola
40. Newman's Own
41. LEGO
42. Fisher-Price
43. Lowe's
44. McDonald's
45. LAY'S
46. Target
47. NIKE
48. Whole Foods
49. Visa
50. AARP

Promotion

Results are promoted through traditional and social media, including a #worldvalue hashtag on Twitter. Brands that make the top rankings promote the results in their own marketing and PR.

More Information

enso.co/worldvalue

PART 6

"Typically, the hardest thing is to simply take the first step."

NEXT STEPS TO GET STARTED

So far in this book, you've learned that a benchmark is any type of comparative, qualitative and/or quantitative data that provides actionable insights. You've also come to appreciate that a benchmark helps you cut through the marketing noise to make your business more valuable and better positioned to attract prospects.

We have also walked you through a specific roadmap for developing a branded benchmark yourself:

1. Define your why

2. Establish a compelling topic

3. Design a methodology

4. Compile the data

5. Summarize your results

6. Partner, promote, and market

7. Follow up, evolve, and extend

You know that you can start small and improve your benchmark as you get reactions and feedback, and as you get better at the entire process.

You've also seen that there are various ways to market your benchmark, no matter how small your promotional budget. You can use traditional media and social media. You can promote the benchmark at events and networking activities. You can partner with those that speak to the similar audience you desire. You are aware of the importance of giving your benchmark a meaningful and memorable name, and the need for a good design and visual assets.

In the previous section, you became familiar with specific examples of branded benchmarks, the various methodologies for developing them, how they are reported and promoted, and how they are used by various stakeholders.

That's a lot to digest and nobody can blame you if you feel overwhelmed.

In this section, we review three over-arching steps you can apply towards having your very own branded benchmark:

1. **Clarify your end user**
   Begin by finding your sweet spot in terms of your clients: Who are your best clients? Who are happy to pay what you charge? And who gladly hire you again and again? Who do you want to attract? Which industry or industry segment can you best serve? What's your ideal client profile?

Considering your best clients is a good place to start because they will give you signals about the types of benchmarks that will capture their interest and serve them best.

2. **Identify your "Onlyness"**
   If you will recall, Onlyness refers to the unique, defendable, and non-competing category of ONE that you occupy. Discovering, clarifying, and articulating your compelling Onlyness will help you determine what kind of benchmark you might want to create.

3. **Review current resources**
   Take a good look at the resources at your disposal that you'll be using in creating and leveraging your branded benchmark. You may already have information and data in your company that others would find helpful.

   Remember to include the networks you can tap into, such as industry organizations, manufacturers and vendors of products you use, and owners of websites and podcasts in your industry. They can be valuable sources of partners and allies. Most of the time, you'll realize that you have more resources than you first thought.

   Typically, the hardest thing is to simply take the first step. If you find that you need help in jumpstarting the process, see the bonus resources to learn more.

BONUS RESOURCES

Transform your business to become a respected industry leader, even if you have little time and money.

Visit **datapointsgold.com** for essential resources to help you start and succeed with your own branded benchmark. We'll support you as you create assets that will raise your profile and boost business profits.

Examples of Tools and Resources Designed to Help You:

- Tips to help you choose the best benchmark topic for you
- Live and on-demand opportunities to learn and apply ideas through webinars and online learning
- Opportunities for Q+A sessions to help you succeed
- No-cost or low-cost ideas to develop, market and publicize your branded benchmark
- How to earn real money with existing clients and others by helping them create their own branded benchmarks
- How to access your own one-on-one guidance to develop and position your branded benchmark
- Downloadable PDF of branded benchmark roadmap
- Ongoing branded benchmark examples we discover to inspire and motivate you

“Analytics, the process of finding and interpreting significant patterns among collected data to assist in making strategic decisions, or sharing actionable insights.”

GLOSSARY

We have provided these definitions for your easy reference. They were compiled from our work experiences, and supplemented from various open sources. In those instances, the source is noted with the definition.

We encourage you to add to the list as you research and develop your own branded benchmark. You can jot your findings on the pages provided for your notes at the end of this book.

A

- **Analytics**, the process of finding and interpreting significant patterns among collected data to assist in making strategic decisions or sharing actionable insights.

- **Assessment**, gathering, reviewing, and analyzing information for a better understanding that can influence an action, decision, or conclusion.

- **Average**, the arithmetic mean between multiple quantities or numbers—the sum of the numbers divided by the amount of numbers present.

- **Artificial Intelligence, (AI)**, an area of computer science that emphasizes the creation of intelligent machines that work and react like humans. Activities computers with artificial intelligence are designed to include: Speech Recognition and Machine Learning. *(techopedia.com - adapted)*

B

- **Benchmarking**, using an industry's leading performance metrics and best practices as the standard for measuring individual business achievement. The broader definition is that a benchmark is any type of qualitative or quantitative data that provides actionable insights and drives decisions.

- **Big Data**, refers to newly accessible sets of information that were previously difficult to analyze due to volume, disparate elements, and/or speed of accumulation.

- **Branded Benchmark**, is distinctive in its core purpose, name, identity and design. It is a benchmark of any type of qualitative or quantitative data that provides actionable insights. It stands out from others, provides value to groups of individuals with a memorable name, clear position in the marketplace, visuals, and more that make it identifiable.

- **Business Intelligence**, the product of research and analysis of "hard" data, typically financial numbers, used to reveal trends and develop strategy.

C

- **Collecting Data**, compiling information for analysis using surveys or other means, such as capturing verbal or numeric information via forms or spreadsheets.

- **Correlation**, a statistical association between two variables that demonstrate either a positive or a negative linear relationship with each other.

- **Customer Intelligence**, information about customer details or behavior, such as demographics or buying preferences.

D

- **Distribution**, as it relates to benchmarking - the computation of all possible intervals of data in a given data set and their frequencies, often displayed in a graph.

- **Design**, as it relates to benchmarking - a detailed outline of how the study/review/survey will take place. A research design will typically include how data is to be collected, which tools will be used, and the intended method for analyzing, reporting the data, and its visual presentation.

- **Data Analytics**, reviewing and analyzing data towards a specific business purpose, insight, and actions. See Analytics

- **Data Science**, the use of algorithms—a particular set of rules applied to calculate an outcome—and computer science theories to gain insights from data sets.

- **Demographics**, population statistics such as age, sex, or income level - the characteristics of human populations for purposes of social studies.

E

- **Establishing the Focus**, defining and setting the subject, range, or particular type of measurement, analysis, and information to be investigated, researched, or developed.

- **Engage**, to motivate, require, inspire, or compel interaction with information, environments, individuals, an organization, or some other element.

F

- **Findings**, facts and figures collected from a given data set from which to draw conclusions and take informed action.

- **Framework**, a basic structure or set of connected steps that guide a system or concept, usually serving as a guide or path from a beginning to a desired result.

G

- **Graphics**, relative to informaiton, are common ways data is displayed such as infographics, bar graphs, images, and specific depiction with typography to convey a concept.

- **General Data Protection Regulations (GDPR)**, is the European Union legislation as of May 2018 that requires protection of personal information retained on individuals.

- **Governance**, managing, overseeing, controlling access to or a set-up to maintain a system or processes, including establishing pertinent policies and guidelines.

H

- **High-Low Ranges — High-Low Method**, a way of attempting to separate out fixed and variable costs given a limited amount of data in cost accounting. The high-low method involves taking the highest level of activity and the lowest level of activity, and comparing the total costs at each level. *(investopedia.com)*

I

- **Infographics**, visual representation of data that lends meaning to verbal or numeric elements, such as an annotated pie chart or line graph. See Graphics

- **Insight**, a realization about the nature of business elements that puts data into perspective, such as the detection of correlations or trends. The goal is to draw conclusions that lead to or inspire action.

- **Information Technology, or IT**, computing technology and the application of its components, including hardware, software, networking, and Internet platforms.

J

- **Joining Data Sets**, integrating data from two or more sources to provide broader insights, particularly used with Big Data.

K

- **Key Performance Indicators (KPI)**, business statistics such as cash flow, sales revenue, and return on investment that are measured periodically to reveal how well a company meets objectives over time.

L

- **Leverage**, is a strategy of using resources, contacts, or other assets to increase the potential return of an investment, efforts or actions. *(businessdictionary.com - adapted)*

M

- **Measurement**, is the assignment of a number to a characteristic of an object or event, which can be compared with other objects or events.

- **Mean**, the "average" number; found by adding all data points and dividing by the number of data points. See Average. *(khanacademy.org)*

- **Median**, the middle number; found by ordering all data points and picking out the one in the middle (or if there are two middle numbers, taking the mean of those two numbers). *(khanacademy.org)*

- **Market Research**, an assessment of how viable a new product or service will be based on the results of testing, surveys, discoveries, focus groups, and more.

- **Machine Learning**, is a method of data analysis that automates analytical model building. It is a branch of artificial intelligence based on the idea that systems can learn from data, identify patterns and make decisions with minimal human intervention. *(sas.com)*

- **Methodology**, set of rules or procedures applied to solve different, defined problems within the scope of a particular discipline. *(businessdictionary.com)*

N

- **Net Promoter Score (NPS)**, a metric that reveals the degree of customer willingness to recommend a company, organization or brand.

O

- **Original Research**, information discovery, investigation, and analysis conducted on proprietary or previously unavailable subject pools (primary research) or based upon previous findings (secondary research). It is often data-driven.

P

- **Probability**, the measurement and determination of how likely an event is to occur.

- **Predictive Modeling**, an analytical process that determines the statistical probability of outcomes.

- **Prescriptive**, as it relates to benchmarking - analysis that generates potential actions to satisfy predictive results, as well as the data-backed consequences of each one.

Q

- **Quick Tests**, tests that don't cost much to design, are based on some estimated idea for how the system could fail (risk-based) and don't take much prior knowledge in order to apply. *(kenst.com)*

R

- **Regression Testing**, repeats previous tests to determine functionality after a change has been made.

- **Regression Modeling**, a statistical process that reveals how the value of a dependent variable changes when one of its independent variables changes and others do not.

S

- **Sampling**, a statistical process that gleans representative information from a targeted group.

- **Summary**, an overview that describes a subject, theme, methodology, and/or results but not specific details.

- **Segmentation**, breaking down a homogenous target market into its identifiable parts, such as needs, wants, or preferences.

- **Survey**, human research conducted verbally or via written questions and answers to gather facts or assess opinions.

T

- **Tracking**, to observe, monitor, or record the course or path of an activity, process, service, or object.

- **Trends**, the general movement over time of a statistically detectable change, also a statistical curve reflecting such a change. *(Merriam-Webster Dictionary)*

U

- **Utility**, in economics utility is simply a function of the satisfaction that a consumer experiences from a product or service. Utility is an important factor in decision-making and product choices. However, it can be a challenge to incorporate utility into predictive models because it varies among consumers for the same product, and it can be influenced by other factors, such as price, availability of alternatives and more. *(investopedia – adapted)*

V

- **Visualization**, graphical or illustrative images that depict a set of tracked data, comparisons or ideas in order to convey a particular story or goal. *(dictionary.com – adapted)*

W

- **White Paper**, marketing tool or expression of a point-of-view in the form of a report on the technology or concepts underlying a product or system and on how it will benefit the customer or reader. *(businessdictionary.com – adapted)*

X+Y

- **X and Y**, data dimensions or coordinates presented along axes where Y depends on X—independent variable X is represented horizontally and dependent variable Y is represented vertically.

Z

- **Zone pricing**, the process of setting prices for goods or services based on the location where they will be offered for sale to consumers. *(businessdictionary.com)*

- **Zero sum game**, in decision theory, a situation where one or more participants' gain (loss) equals the loss (gain) of other participants. Thus, a gain (loss) for one results in a loss (gain) for another. *(businessdictionary.com)*

- **Zag**, in brand strategy, a maneuver that creates a point of compelling radical differentiation that results in a powerful competitive advantage. *(Marty Neumeier – The Dictionary of Brand - adapted)*

REFERENCES

Page 4

[1] blogs.gartner.com/doug-laney/tobins-q-a-evidence-of-informations-real-market-value-2

Page 13

[2] orbitmedia.com/blog/how-to-make-a-survey

Page 18

[3] bain.com/insights/management-tools-benchmarking

Page 23

[4] netpromoter.com/know

Page 53

[5] interbrand.com/views/heart-mind-the-beauty-of-naming-is-in-the-balance

Page 54

[6] martyneumeier.com/strong-vs-weak-names

Page 56

[7] martyneumeier.com/the-onlyness-test

Page 57

[8] martyneumeier.com/the-onlyness-test

All other sources are noted within the pertinent text.

ABOUT THE AUTHORS

LinkedIn.com/in/AnaeziModu

Anaezi Modu is founder and CEO of REBRAND™ and producer of the REBRAND 100® Global Awards, the highest recognition and benchmark for effective brand transformations in the world. She speaks, writes and consults on brand change driven by business goals, including M&A and spin-offs in developed and emerging markets.

One of Anaezi's goals is to help small businesses leverage some tools and strategies that global brands with much greater resources apply for competitive advantage. Data Points Gold, focused on small businesses, results from that goal.

Anaezi integrates brand insights, design and strategy to achieve business goals. She accomplishes this through publishing, research, teaching opportunities such as at Harvard Graduate School of Design, speaking invitations including a keynote presentation in Madrid at the invitation of ICOGRADA and Spain's Ministry of Innovation and Design, and for various professional organizations and board positions.

Prior to founding REBRAND™ Anaezi was Senior Vice President, Information Architect and Brand Experience at Bank of America. She holds a degree in Architecture and Urban Planning from Princeton University, and a Master of Architecture and Design from Harvard University's Graduate School of Design, integrating course work at Massachusetts Institute of Technology.

ABOUT THE AUTHORS

LinkedIn.com/in/AnziyaBundu

Anziya Bundu's quantitative and analytical mind combined with technical, artistic, and innovative skills drive her unique insights from data design and benchmarking strategy. She is experienced in analyzing data and visual content for technology, fashion, and lifestyle brands.

That experience has been balanced with past roles in IT divisions of financial services and technology firms. She has developed regression models based on research to forecast trends and impacts of fashion industry diversity and strategy.

Anziya holds a Bachelor of Science in Economics with minors in International Affairs and Sociology from Northeastern University. Her areas of focus include data mining, economic regression modeling, predictive analytics insights, visual digital strategy, and technology tools for quality assurance testing and automation.

ABOUT REBRAND

LinkedIn.com/company/REBRAND

REBRAND™ is the world's leading platform for case studies and programs on effective brand transformations. Its renowned REBRAND 100® Global Awards, juried by an esteemed panel of international designers, business leaders and educators, is the highest recognition for brand rebuilding and redesign in business. It is the first and only global program of its kind.

Having reached over 63 countries in 40+ industries, and featured in such media as The Wall Street Journal, BBC, Fast Company, articles and books, the selected case studies are an unrivaled global library of transformed brands for business reference. REBRAND 100 is a prestigious ranking and an important benchmark for other companies managing their brand assets.

REBRAND has several sub-brands and alliance initiatives underway. One of those is the development of BUILDPLAY™, the creator of the BUILDPLAY Digital Index™. BUILDPLAY tracks the digital performance, brand reputation and global megatrends for built environment industries that include architecture, construction, engineering (A/E/C), commercial real estate and property services firms.

Visit: rebrand.com
Visit: buildplay.com

NOTES

NOTES

www.ingramcontent.com/pod-product-compliance
Lightning Source LLC
Chambersburg PA
CBHW080423060326
40689CB00019B/4363
* 9 7 8 0 9 9 9 0 8 2 3 7 9 *